W9-DDW-677

French Provincial Cookery

COLETTE BLACK

FRENCH PROVINCIAL COOKERY

Illustrated by Janice Cowen

THE CROWELL-COLLIER PRESS

First Crowell-Collier Press Edition 1963

Library of Congress Catalog Card Number: 63-7148

Hecho en los E.E.U.U.
Printed in the United States of America

Contents

French Provincial Cookery

The Food of Provincial France

THE FOOD OF FRANCE is undoubtedly the most interesting and varied of any country in the world, indicative of a high degree of culinary invention on the part of the French people. If it be true that each nation gets the food it deserves, surely the Gallic people are the most individualistic and varied nation on the globe.

Most Americans visit France in a pattern that has worn the trail smooth by repetition. Almost everyone visits Paris, a large proportion goes to the French Riviera, a small segment sight-sees for a few days in the château country of the Loire. A French Tourist Office survey of the travel habits of tourists indicates that the vast majority of Americans rarely deviates from this well-worn pattern, and thus never gets to see the delightful rural countryside of France. One who has traveled the regular tourist route through Paris, the Riviera, and the Loire Valley eats very well indeed, but it would be erroneous to assume that, by doing so, one gains a complete knowledge of the tremendous range and extent of French cuisine. There are those who say that Parisian cookery, delicious and elaborate as it may be, cannot hope to measure up to the home-style, flavorsome food of the provinces.

This book is intended to introduce the reader to the wonders of French cookery as it is practiced in the small towns and villages of the Gallic countryside. It contains many of the classic, everyday dishes that have made French food famous throughout the world; no single book could even aspire to do more than present some of the more famous preparations, for French provincial cooking consists of many thousands of dishes. Indeed, many individual provinces of France have a thousand or more separate dishes themselves, and thus a complete series of books would be required to make a proper presentation of provincial cookery.

The main point to bear in mind about provincial cooking is that it is done by housewives—the wives of peasants, farmers, shopkeepers, and small businessmen. It consists of the

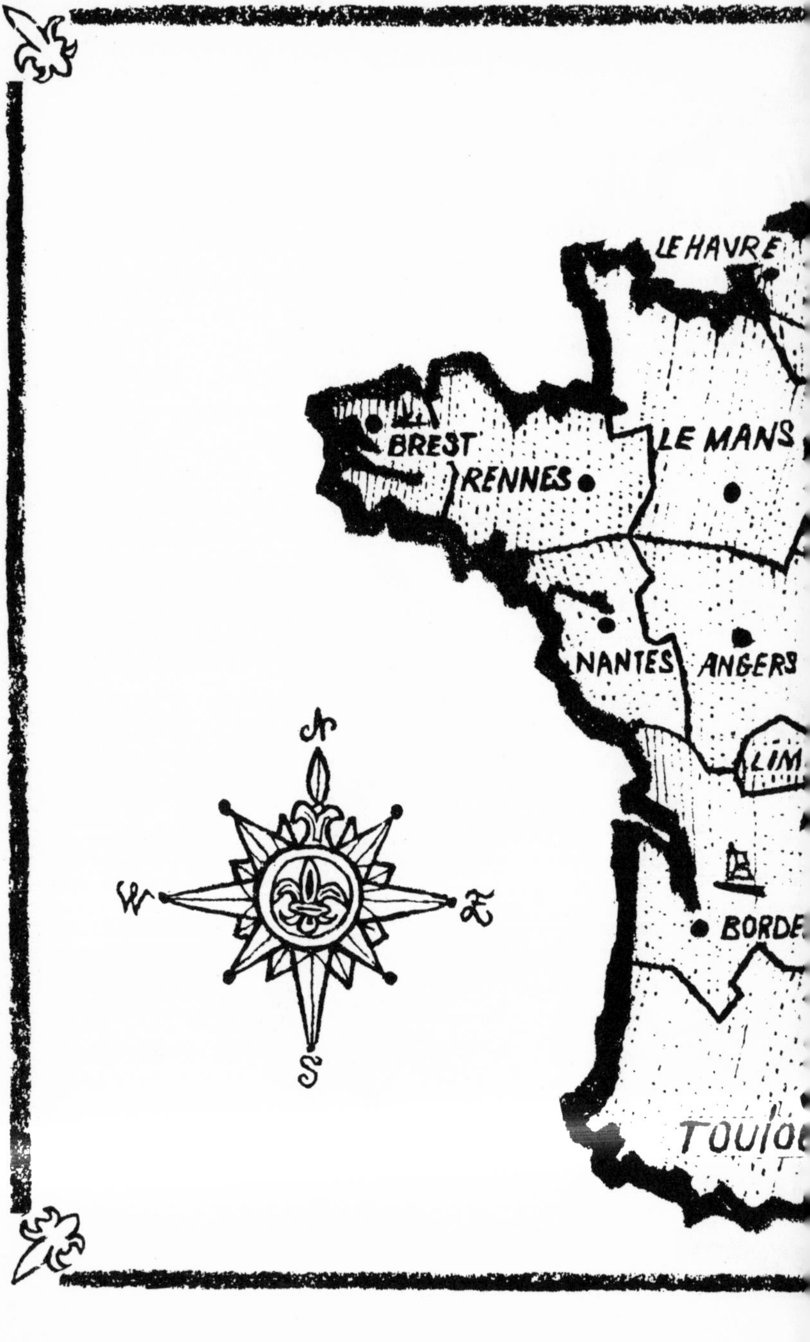

N

W

E

S

LE HAVRE

BREST

RENNES

LE MANS

NANTES

ANGERS

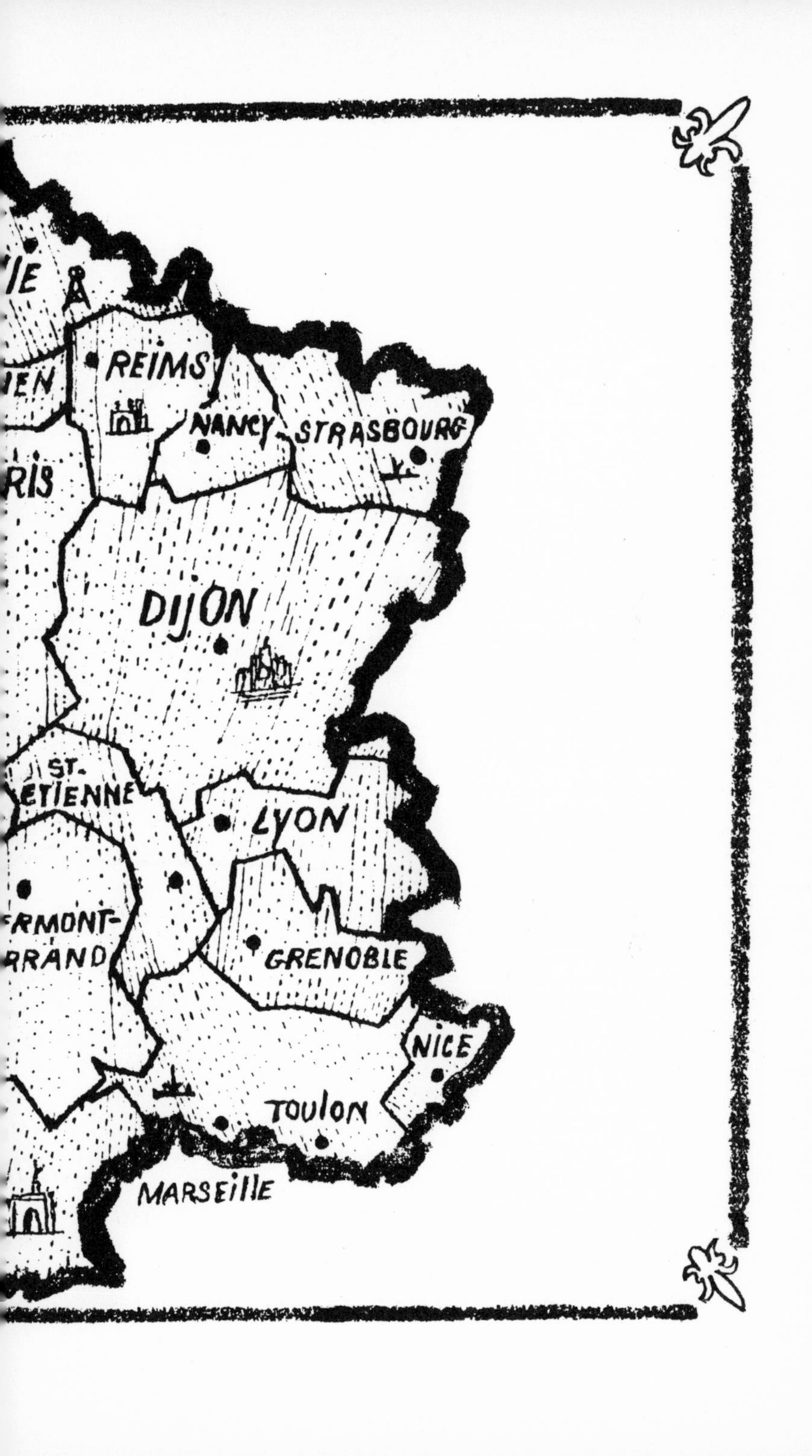
REIMS
NANCY
STRASBOURG
DIJON
ST. ETIENNE
LYON
GRENOBLE
NICE
TOULON
MARSEILLE

everyday dishes that almost everyone in France eats as daily fare. The first requirement of these provincial dishes is that the ingredients should be readily available and not too expensive for daily fare; the second requirement is that the dish should be easily prepared by a good basic cook. If the dish fulfills these requirements and has become a stand-by throughout all of France, the dish is considered as a part of French *cuisine bourgeoise,* that is, part of the everyday dishes served everywhere in France. *Bourgeoise* literally means middle class, but the reference is not completely accurate at the present time, because every Frenchman, rich or poor, peasant or Parisian, eats this type of food daily, as a matter of routine. However, these dishes did originate with the middle class, that backbone of the Gallic social structure, and have since become the standard daily fare for 45,000,000 present-day Frenchmen. In addition to *cuisine bourgeoise,* France is renowned for its provincial cookery, *cuisine régionale,* the term having reference to the special dishes created in any of the various provinces of France. Just as the United States is divided into states, so is France divided into departments, or provinces. Without exception, each province has developed its own provincial style, usually based upon ingredients grown or otherwise available in that province. For example, in Normandy, which fronts onto the Atlantic Ocean, the cuisine relies heavily upon fish because the ingredients are fresh, moderately priced, and always available. Similarly, in Burgundy, much of the cookery uses the local wines, because wine of the district is always at hand.

The *cuisine régionale* was not necessarily simple, because frequently the dishes took advantage of expensive, scarce items such as *pâté de foie gras* and truffles, as is the situation in the Périgord district of southwestern France. When the dishes of the *cuisine régionale* reached acceptable heights of sophistication and excellence in the opinion of French gourmets, particularly the pace-setters of Paris, they became a part of the classic cuisine of France. As such, they fitted into the third category of French cuisine generally called *haute cuisine,* which literally translates into high cuisine, but more correctly refers to the standard, accepted, classic cuisine of

France. An example of a dish which originally was a regional creation in Strasbourg, that ancient city of Alsace near the German border, is *dinde Strasbourgeoise,* turkey prepared with chicken livers and truffles; it first came into existence as a holiday dish in Strasbourg, but its reputation grew rapidly and soon gourmets in Paris adopted it, and it became, and still remains, one of the foremost preparations of the *haute cuisine.*

Throughout this book, therefore, appear recipes that might be classified as either *cuisine bourgeoise* or *cuisine régionale,* depending chiefly upon whether they are generally prepared all through France, or just in particular regions. As a rule, where a recipe appears (for example) simply as *blanquette de veau,* without further qualification, it indicates that the particular dish is served everywhere in France. However, where the name of the dish is followed by that of a province or provincial city, it means that the dish is regional in nature, as is the case with such dishes as *pommes de terre à la Lyonnaise,* or *boeuf Bourguignonne;* in the first dish, the derivation indicates a specialty of the city of Lyons, whereas the second preparation originated in the region of Burgundy, rather than a particular city of that province.

Very few tourists have the time necessary to tour all of the provinces of France, but even those who have never been abroad can enjoy the remarkable ingenuity and inventiveness shown by the provincial cooks of France. Starting at the coast, the province of Brittany is a good beginning, because it is closest to the United States. This is a district of rocky coastlines, crashing green waves dashing upon the craggy beaches, and an individualistic fisherfolk, speaking a distinctive linguistic variation of the French language. Fish and shellfish are exceptional; with everything they eat, the Bretons drink their locally made cider, because no wine is produced here. Much of the cuisine is based upon sauces made with cider, usually with the addition of cream and butter, for Brittany is also a dairy region. As an example, *poulet Breton* might be cited, a delightful dish made of chicken in cider and cream. Noteworthy here is a famous dessert, the delicious *crêpes* of the region.

In adjacent Normandy, the fish is also remarkable, and fish soups and stews are exceptional. The *sole Normande* is a classic dish, consisting of sole prepared with a shrimp and mushroom sauce. With much grazing land near the sea, the lambs that feed upon the salt-marsh grasses develop a distinctive quality, so that the diner can recognize the lamb instantly; lamb of this sort is called *mouton de pré-salé,* salt-marsh lamb. In the city of Caen there is a famous dish called *tripe à la mode de Caen,* or tripe as it is prepared in that city.

Alsace and Lorraine, those two provinces of France which have changed hands frequently between France and Germany over the past century, have many exceptional dishes. *Quiche Lorraine,* that renowned cheese pie which is served as an appetizer, originated here; another variation is *tarte à l'oignon,* an appetizer onion pie. *Foie gras,* goose liver, is packed here, and many of the great regional dishes are prepared with it, notably the turkey, as previously mentioned. *Pflütters,* a potato preparation, and the *galette Strasbourgeoise,* a kind of raisin cake, are worth mentioning. Poultry and meats are cooked with sauerkraut, sometimes with the local Riesling wines. None of the Alsatian wines is terribly good, but they are all drinkable and pleasant, all light white wines. Sylvaner, Riesling, and Traminer are the ones to remember.

In Franche-Comté, to the immediate south and also adjacent to Germany, the people are fond of game, particularly the wild birds of the forests like *bécasse,* woodcock. From the streams come trout, but best of all are the small river crayfish, pink and white, and filled with delicious shellfish flavor. The peasants, and the townsfolk too, for that matter, look forward to a holiday; they head for the forests and pick the wild mushrooms they know so well. Forget about cultivated, snowy-white, and comparatively tasteless mushrooms! Wild mushrooms are something entirely different, filled with the subtle aroma of the woods. They are *morilles, chanterelles, oronges,* and of *course* the standard *cèpes,* all delicious and worth spending a day in the woods searching for. There are recipes furnished for two excellent Franche-Comté dishes

—*feuilleté au fromage* (cheese pastry), and *coq en pâte* (chicken in pastry).

Burgundy, or *Bourgogne* as the French have it, is one of the two most important wine districts of France (the other being Bordeaux). Some of the most expensive wines in the world grow in the narrow strip of wineland that stretches south from Dijon, and naturally the cuisine is intertwined with the fine wines of Burgundy. The dishes prepared with wine in this province are so numerous that a separate book could be written on them alone, but of special interest are *coq au vin* (chicken in wine), *entrecôte grillé* (prepared with red wine), and *boeuf Bourguignonne* (a beef stew made with red wine). Burgundy is famous for its snail dishes, a distinctive fish chowder called *pochouse,* and a simple dish filled with flavor, *boeuf bouilli,* boiled beef.

Burgundy's wines should satisfy any taste. There are ordinary wines at very fair prices produced here, but the demand for Burgundy always exceeds the supply and prices seem to edge up steadily. Burgundy is famous for its great wines, and these, unfortunately, sell at quite high prices. The acknowledged king of Burgundy is undoubtedly the heavy, full-bodied wine of Romanée-Conti. The next group includes (although not necessarily in the order of excellence) such wines as Clos Vougeot, Chambertin, Richebourg, Musigny, and La Tâche. These are all red wines, with world-wide reputations. In the white wines, Burgundy's best is Le Montrachet, a superb wine, perfectly balanced. Also worthy of mention among the white wines is Pouilly-Fuissé, a rather unusual product with a distinctively "flinty" taste, the word "flinty" being used to describe an odd, slightly metallic quality of the wine.

In Nivernais, the accent is upon vegetables. The cooking here is perhaps not so distinctive as in adjacent provinces, for the Nivernais are not the outstanding cooks of France, but they have a wide assortment of excellent vegetables soups, illustrated in this volume by *légumes à la Nivernaise.* Carrots, in particular, are a local specialty: witness *potage crème à la Nivernaise,* a creamed carrot soup. Another point of distinction is the premium placed upon that lowly animal, the pig, and its surprisingly superb products, especially ham, which the Nivernais use to good advantage in *jambon Nivernais* and *saupiquet*. With the ham, don't forget to make some potato pancakes, called *la râpée* in this province. The wine of this district is Pouilly-Fumé (not to be confused with Pouilly-Fuissé mentioned previously); it is a green and gold wine with a clean, dry taste, very vaguely like a dry martini, but much less alcoholic.

Orléanais is the provincial region which includes the Loire River Valley and the château country, one of the few districts that tourists are likely to visit. The cuisine of the region is good, but not inventive, other than for game and Loire River fish, especially the delicate, pale salmon. There are no important wines produced in Orléanais and in fact, there are only a very few local, rather thin wines which are pleasant to drink while on a trip through this province, but which are soon forgotten.

The Touraine is an extension of the Loire River-château country of Orléanais, filled with quiet green fields and a contemplative stretch of riverbank along the Loire. The region, alas, like Orléanais has few great food specialties, although the river fish is extremely good. The local people are particularly fond of *pâté,* that most delicious of all liver preparations, and also of *rillettes,* a rather coarse version of *pâté*. The district is noted for its prunes, and these are likely to be found in some unusual combinations—pork and prunes, for example. Vegetables grow well in the Touraine, and an outstanding vegetable soup is called *soupe Tourangelle*. There are wines galore in this province, and driving along from one château to another, one will encounter literally dozens of villages, each featuring its own special type. However, of them all, three stand out. Vouvray is a fairly good white wine, ideal with fish, although it is just slightly sweet. Among the red wines, Chinon and Bourgueil are quite well known; they are somewhat thin and uneven, but very pleasant to drink with the local food.

In Poitou, facing the Atlantic Ocean, the countryside is interesting, but it is rare to encounter American travelers wandering along this stretch of France. On the other hand, the French like to come here for their summer vacations, and during August the beaches are filled with vacationing members of the French *bourgeoisie.* Butter and cream are employed with a lavish hand (perhaps even a heavy one) in Poitou, and perhaps a little wine, too. Everything is smooth, rich, and unctuous, and that's the way they like their food prepared in this province. The *escalope Poitevine* is an example of the province's classic cookery style; the *tourtière Poitevine* is just about as good as a chicken pie can ever hope to be.

Limousin and Auvergne are adjacent to each other, and have much in common, gastronomically speaking. These regions are ideal for farming and the raising of cattle and poultry for the market. Fruits abound in the orchards, rivers have their fish, and forests their game and mushrooms for the knowing. In Limousin, they prepare a marvelous cherry dessert called *clafoutis;* in the Auvergne, there is an excellent vegetable soup called *soupe Auvergnate,* and a wide choice of poultry dishes. No important wines are produced here, but the local cheeses are exceptional.

Lyonnais, it is said, has the best food of all France. Centrally located, the province receives food from all over the country, and French gourmets claim that Lyons, at least on a percentage-of-population basis, has more gourmets and fine restaurants than Paris. Without taking sides, the fact remains that the cuisine of this province is so extensive and varied that one might well eat only local dishes, day after day, for many weeks without repeating a single preparation. One thing distinguishes Lyonnais cooking from any other provincial style and that is the liberal use of onions, which appear in many dishes, even where its use might well be questioned. *Pommes de terre à la Lyonnaise,* potatoes with onions, is a perfect example of this. This is a province of serious eaters, and no nonsense about little snacks and appetizers. They like *tournedos* (center cuts of beef), *ris de veau* (sweetbreads), and *boeuf sauté,* as well as other hearty dishes. Lyonnais is noted for one important wine, Beaujolais. It is a good wine, low-priced and popular, and just the sort of wine likely to be served in a carafe with your meal. It is a wine without fuss or feathers, but one that people always like.

Bresse is famed for its chicken, snowy-white of breast and of a delicacy rarely encountered. French menus boast of featuring *poulet de Bresse,* chicken grown in the province of Bresse, for there is nothing finer raised anywhere in the world. But Bresse boasts of more than its chicken. It is a province noted for its good living—cheese, truffles, mushrooms, wild game birds, and delicate fish from the streams, are all to be had in abundance in Bresse. The local wines are light and pleasant, but none of them is well known and they are difficult to find outside of the province.

Savoy, in the east central part of France, partly borders on Switzerland and Italy; it is a mountainous province, notably near Chamonix, and is one of the most ruggedly beautiful of all regions of the nation. Cheeses are excellent here, for this is grazing land, crowded with cattle on the rolling land. The woods conceal wild game, mushrooms, and the best tiny wood strawberries of France, those delectable *fraises des bois,* an absolute delight to everyone but the person who has to pick them over. In this book, there are recipes for two notable Savoy dishes—*omelette à la Savoyarde,* an omelet with potatoes and onions, and a good spongecake, the *biscuit de Savoie.*

Dauphiny, just to the south of Savoy, is mountainous and has some stupendous scenery, but the cuisine is less exhilarating, although the food is hearty and pleasing. If there is one dish which expresses Dauphiny, it is the *gratin,* a potato and cheese dish ideal on a cold winter's day when the appetite demands something substantial and filling. There are some remarkable wines grown in the southwestern portion of the province, especially Côte Rôtie and Hermitage. The red wines are full-bodied, heart-warming, high in alcohol, but just slightly crude to the taste. Nonetheless, they are wines of importance, and like Beaujolais, almost everyone seems to find them appealing.

Périgord is a tiny province, one filled with good eating. The local people are particularly fond of *charcuterie,* that is, delicatessen meats. The shops of this region feature a range of sausages that bewilders the senses. However, the great delicacy of this region is the truffle, that mysterious tuber-like growth with the concentrated taste and flavor of mush-rooms, so prized by gourmets. Truffles are found by skilled pigs and dogs, who dig around under oak trees until they un-cover the delectable morsel. In Périgord, truffles are used in a tremendous variety of dishes, so that breakfast scrambled eggs often contain a piece or two. Truffles are not for the average person (except on special occasions), for they command a fabulous price in the market.

In the southwest is Bordeaux, the other, besides Burgundy, of the two great wine districts of France. Wine is used by everyone in cooking and the range of dishes prepared *à la Bordelaise,* with Bordeaux wine, is just short of fantastic. An *entrecôte Bordelaise,* a steak prepared with beef marrow and red wine, is classic all over France and the rest of the world, for that matter. The local people like stews and casseroles, and there are recipes in this book for *veau en casserole,* veal casserole, and *ragoût de boeuf,* beef stew. The Bordeaux red wines are, of course, absolutely superb. The great "château" wines are Lafite, Latour, Haut-Brion, and Margaux. But of course, Bordeaux has literally hundreds of important wines, and it is not necessary to drink those from the most ex-pensive and renowned vineyards in order to enjoy the pleas-ures of Bordeaux wines. Among the white Bordeaux wines, Château d'Yquem, an outstanding sweet wine produced in the tiny region of Sauternes, is often considered the greatest of all white dessert wines.

Gascony and Guyenne, in the extreme southwestern portion of the country, have excellent fresh-water fish, and of course, there is wild game in the hills. The district features com-paratively few important specialties, however, although the cookery style is appetizing and homelike. Cooking is usually with fat, sometimes with oil, and only occasionally with butter. The hungry peasants of this region are very fond of soups and stews, hearty fare, rather than ethereal creations designed to tempt the capricious appetite. No need to tempt their unfailing appetites in this region! The *estouffat,* beef stew, is illustrative of Gascony cookery; the *potage Landaise* is a sort of noodle soup. Incidentally, Landaise has reference to Landes, a small *département* within Gascony.

Roussillon and Languedoc, fronting onto the Mediterranean, naturally feature seafood in their cuisine. What could be more delightful than a cold *langouste,* the spiny clawless lobster found in the Mediterranean, accompanied by a glass of cool white wine? But *langouste,* alas, are rarely encountered in the United States, and if they were available, could never have that peculiar and distinctive salty quality, indicating that they are fresh out of the water. Another great feature of the local cooking involves the humble bean, which is prepared in the best possible way, as a *cassoulet.* From village to village through the region, every housewife has her own recipe, some adding duck or goose, others feeling that beans and meat are enough. The recipe for *cassoulet de Castelnaudary* is an example of how there can be a variation upon a good original theme.

Is the best last? In this case, many Frenchmen (and not a few tourists) might agree that Provence has one of the most original and intriguing cuisines of any province of France. Provence covers the entire French Riviera, that glamorous stretch of coast which has become the favorite of the international set. From Marseille to the Italian border, the entire luxury coast, including simple fishing villages, the deluxe beach resorts, and a magnificent, rocky coastline—all these make up fabulous Provence, the sunniest, warmest part of France. Around Marseille, the cooking is strongly influenced by olive oil, seafood, and olives. Here is the home of *bouillabaisse,* that fascinating soup-stew. Duck with olives, *canard aux olives,* is indicative of the Provençal manner of using olives in every possible way. All through this region, vegetables grow to magnificent size and lustrousness, eggplants shining in purple splendor, string beans in even blue-green rows, tomatoes so red that one is drawn to them because of the brilliant color. All vegetables are cooked with oil and garlic, *à la Niçoise,* or in the style of Nice, the largest city of Provence. It might be mentioned that Nice and the surrounding area were once part of Italy, and only joined France about a century ago. The Italian influence is still strong, and to this day, a Niçoise accent has a slight Italian quality to it. In cookery, too, the Italian influence is noticeable, and the people of this region are extremely fond of *pasta* and Italian food. The classic appetizer called *pissaladière Niçoise* is nothing more than a French version of an Italian *pizza*. It is best to like garlic if one visits Provence, because it flavors soups, stews, omelets, meat, and fish. The wine-lover will find two pleasing wines in Provence, the light white wines of Cassis, which so well accompany a fish soup like *bouillabaisse*, and also the *rosé* wines of Bellet, which by their nature are the perfect accompaniment for the spicy food of Provence.

You'll find great pleasure in eating the provincial food of France. With it, have the enjoyment of a glass of good wine.

COLETTE BLACK

Appetizers

Appetizers

OIGNONS À LA MONÉGASQUE

Onions in Raisin Sauce, Monaco Fashion

1½ pounds small white onions
4 tablespoons olive oil
1½ cups water
½ cup wine vinegar
3 tablespoons tomato paste
1 bay leaf
¼ teaspoon marjoram
2 tablespoons sugar
½ cup seedless raisins
1½ teaspoons salt
½ teaspoon freshly ground black pepper

Pick onions of uniform size. Peel them. Heat the oil in a saucepan, add onions, and toss until coated. Add the water, vinegar, tomato paste, bay leaf, marjoram, sugar, raisins, salt and pepper and bring to a boil. Cook over low heat, covered, 30 minutes, shaking the pan frequently. Chill. Serve as a vegetable or hors d'oeuvre.

Serves 6-8.

PISSALADIÈRE NIÇOISE

Onion Appetizer, Nice Style

1 package hot roll mix
1⅛ cups olive oil
3 pounds onions, thinly sliced
2 leeks, white part only, thinly sliced
2 cloves garlic, chopped
1¼ teaspoons salt
½ teaspoon freshly ground black pepper
1 small can anchovy fillets
Pitted black olives

Prepare the hot roll mix as package directs, then knead into it ⅛ cup oil; roll it out very thin and fit into an 11- by 17-inch baking pan.

Heat the remaining oil in a skillet; sauté the onions, leeks, garlic, salt and pepper 25 minutes, mixing frequently. Drain and cool. Spread onion mixture evenly over dough and arrange the anchovy fillets in a lattice design, making about 2-inch squares. Put a black olive in center of each square. Bake in a preheated 350° oven 30 minutes. Cut into squares and serve hot.

Makes about 45.

QUICHE LORRAINE

Bacon-Custard Pie

18 slices of bacon
9-inch pastry shell
4 eggs
½ teaspoon salt
⅛ teaspoon nutmeg
2 cups light cream
2 tablespoons butter

Preheat the oven to 375°. Fry the bacon crisp. Drain well. Arrange in an overlapping design on the bottom of the pie shell. Beat together the eggs, salt, nutmeg and cream. Pour over the bacon. Dot with the butter. Bake 40 minutes or until delicately browned and set. Let stand ½ hour before serving warm.

Quiche Lorraine au Fromage

Arrange 12 thin slices of Gruyère or Swiss cheese over the bacon. Pour the custard over it and bake as directed.

TARTE À L'OIGNON ALSACIENNE

Alsatian Onion Tart

2 tablespoons butter
2 cups sliced onions or scallions (green onions)
3 eggs
1 cup cream
Salt, freshly ground black pepper
1 unbaked 9-inch pastry shell
1 slice of bacon, cut in tiny squares

Melt the butter in a skillet and sauté the onions until soft and yellow. Beat eggs and add to them the cream, sautéed onions, and salt and pepper to taste. Mix well and pour into pie shell. Sprinkle top with bacon and bake in a 400° oven 30 minutes or until set. Serve hot.

Serves 6-8.

FEUILLETÉ AU FROMAGE FRANCHE-COMTÉ

Cheese Pastry

½ recipe Puff Pastry (see recipe)
¾ cup butter
⅔ cup flour
4 cups warm milk
6 egg yolks, beaten
1 pound Swiss cheese, grated
Salt, freshly ground white pepper

Roll out puff pastry and cut into 3 strips, each measuring about 4 inches by 12 inches. Bake in a preheated 375° oven until puffed and brown, about 45 minutes.

Melt butter in a saucepan and stir in flour until smooth. Slowly add milk, stirring constantly. Cook, stirring steadily, until smooth and thick. Cool 5 minutes. Stir in egg yolks and a little less than 1 pound of cheese. Season with salt and pepper. Sandwich puff pastry layers with cheese mixture. Sprinkle top with remaining grated cheese and bake in a 450° oven 5 minutes. Serve at once.

Serves 6-9.

GRATIN DE CHAMPIGNONS LANGUEDOCIEN

Stuffed Mushrooms

1 pound firm white large mushrooms
1 cup boiling water
¾ teaspoon salt
2 teaspoons lemon juice
3 tablespoons butter
1 shallot, chopped, or ½ onion, chopped
5 tablespoons finely diced ham
1 cup dry white wine
Foie gras
1¼ cups Béchamel sauce (see recipe)
½ cup grated Parmesan cheese

Remove stems from mushrooms. Wash stems and caps thoroughly. Put caps in a saucepan with the boiling water, salt, lemon juice, and half the butter. Cover and cook 3 minutes. Drain caps and arrange in a buttered shallow baking dish, underside up.

Melt the remaining butter in a skillet and sauté the shallot and ham. Chop the mushroom stems and add; continue sautéing for several minutes over high heat. Add wine and simmer 20 minutes or until the mixture is the right consistency for stuffing. Fill mushroom caps with stuffing and top each with a thin slice of foie gras. Cover with Béchamel sauce, sprinkle with cheese, and brown in a hot oven.

Serves 4.

ANCHOIADE

Anchovy Canapés

1 can anchovy fillets
3 cloves garlic, chopped
2 tablespoons bread crumbs, soaked in water
¼ teaspoon freshly ground black pepper
2 tablespoons olive oil
¼ teaspoon wine vinegar
10 slices of French bread, lightly toasted

Pound the undrained anchovy fillets and garlic in a mortar, or chop very fine. Press moisture from bread crumbs and add them to anchovy mixture with the pepper. Mix to a smooth paste and add the oil and wine vinegar. Brush the bread with olive oil, spread thinly with the anchovy mixture, and broil 5 minutes. Serve very hot.

Makes 10 canapés.

PETITES PÂTES À LA PROVENÇALE

Anchovy-Ham Appetizers

1 can anchovy fillets
1 clove garlic, chopped
2 shallots, chopped
4 whole peppercorns
1 teaspoon olive oil
1 tablespoon finely chopped parsley
1 teaspoon chopped chives
1 tablespoon brandy
1 cup chopped ham
2 tablespoons softened butter
1 egg yolk
Dough for 2-crust pie (see Flaky Pastry recipe)

Drain the anchovy fillets and reserve 1 teaspoon of the oil. Put anchovy fillets, garlic, shallots, and peppercorns in a mortar and pound to a paste. Add reserved oil from anchovies, olive oil, parsley, chives, and brandy. Mix well and let stand 10 minutes. Add ham, butter, and egg yolk and mix thoroughly.

Roll out the dough and cut into 3-inch rounds. Place 1 tablespoon of the anchovy-ham filling in the center of each round, wet the edges of the dough, fold over and pinch together. Bake in a 350° oven 20 minutes, or until golden brown.

Makes about 20 turnovers.

ESCARGOTS À LA BOURGUIGNONNE

SNAILS IN GARLIC BUTTER

36 snails
⅓ pound butter
4 tablespoons finely chopped shallots
1 tablespoon minced garlic
3 tablespoons minced parsley
1 teaspoon salt
¼ teaspoon freshly ground black pepper
½ cup dry white wine
¼ cup dry bread crumbs

If fresh snails are not available, buy the canned snails which come with shells separate.

Cream the butter and blend with the shallots, garlic, parsley, salt and pepper. Place a little of this butter in each shell and press a snail into it. Fill shells with remaining butter, packing in firmly. Arrange, filled side up, in 6 snail pans or a baking dish. Pour a little wine over them and sprinkle with bread crumbs. Bake 10 minutes in a 425° oven.

Serves 6.

Soups

Soups

POT-AU-FEU

BEEF-VEGETABLE SOUP

- *1½ pounds rump or chuck of beef*
- *1 marrowbone*
- *1 pound oxtail, cut in 2-inch pieces*
- *4 quarts water*
- *1 onion stuck with 2 cloves*
- *6 leeks, sliced*
- *3 carrots, sliced*
- *1 turnip, diced*
- *2 stalks celery, sliced*
- *2 tablespoons minced parsley*
- *1½ tablespoons salt*
- *3 peppercorns*
- *1 bay leaf*
- *½ teaspoon thyme*
- *2 tablespoons butter*
- *1 small cabbage*
- *Slices of French bread*

Put the beef, marrowbone, and oxtail in a deep pan with the water and bring to a boil. Skim the top. Cook 2 hours over low heat. Add the onion, leeks, carrots, turnip, celery, parsley, salt, peppercorns, bay leaf, and thyme. Cook 30 minutes.

Melt the butter in a pan, cut the cabbage in eighths, and sauté for 5 minutes. Put in soup pan and cook 1 hour. Skim fat off top of soup and adjust seasoning. Dry French bread slices in the oven.

Serve the soup in a tureen. Slice the meat and serve in the soup or on a separate serving platter. Put a slice of French bread in each soup plate and pour soup over it. Parmesan cheese may be sprinkled on top, if desired.

Serves 10-12.

POTAGE LANDAISE

Onion-Noodle Soup

3 tablespoons goose or other fat
4 large onions, finely chopped
3 ounces vermicelli
3 tablespoons tomato paste
1½ quarts beef stock
Grated cheese

Melt the fat in a saucepan and sauté the onions until soft but not brown. Break the vermicelli into small pieces, add to the onions, and cook until the vermicelli begins to color. Add the tomato paste and stock, bring to a boil and cook over low heat 12 minutes. Serve in a tureen and pass cheese separately.

Serves 6.

SOUPE TOURANGELLE

Vegetable Soup, Touraine Style

2 tablespoons butter
6 leeks, white part only, thinly sliced
2 white turnips, peeled and sliced
½ pound lean bacon, finely diced
1 small head cabbage, coarsely shredded
2 quarts beef or chicken stock
1 pound fresh peas, shelled
Thin slices of French bread, toasted

Melt the butter in a saucepan and over low heat sauté the leeks, turnips, bacon, and cabbage, without browning. Add the stock, cover, and cook over low heat 1 hour. Add peas and cook 30 minutes longer. Taste for seasoning. Serve with a slice of toast in each plate.

Serves 6-8.

TOURAIN PÉRIGOURDIN

Vegetable Soup, Périgord Style

2 onions, thinly sliced
2 tablespoons goose or bacon fat
1 clove garlic, mashed
1 tablespoon flour
Salt, freshly ground black pepper
1 pound tomatoes, skinned, seeded, and chopped
Thin slices of French bread, toasted

Lightly brown the onions in the hot fat. Add the garlic and cook a minute or two. Sprinkle with the flour and let brown a little. Blend in 2 tablespoons hot water.

Bring 1½ quarts water to a boil in a saucepan and add the onion mixture, salt and pepper to taste, and the tomatoes. Cook 45 minutes. Taste for seasoning. Put toasted French bread in a tureen or soup plates and pour the soup over it.

Serves 6.

SOUPE NORMANDE

Normandy Vegetable Soup

5 tablespoons butter
1 bunch leeks, thinly sliced
3 small white turnips, thinly sliced
3 potatoes, peeled and thinly sliced
1½ quarts beef stock
½ cup cooked dried lima beans or uncooked fresh lima beans
½ teaspoon salt
¼ teaspoon freshly ground black pepper
1½ cups milk
2 tablespoons heavy cream

Melt 4 tablespoons butter in a heavy pan, add leeks and turnips, and cook over low heat 5 minutes. Add potatoes and cook 5 minutes but do not brown. Add stock and lima beans and season with the salt and pepper. Mix in milk and cook over very low heat until vegetables are tender. Stir in the remaining tablespoon butter and the cream and serve.

Serves 6-8.

SOUPE AUVERGNATE

Vegetable Soup as prepared in the Auvergne

8 cups water
1½ teaspoons salt
¼ teaspoon freshly ground black pepper
4 carrots, sliced
2 turnips, sliced
1 2-pound cabbage, quartered
1 clove garlic
4 small potatoes, peeled and sliced
4 tablespoons diced lean bacon
Slices of French bread, toasted

Put in a saucepan the water, salt, pepper, carrots, turnips, cabbage, and garlic. Bring to a boil and simmer until vegetables are half cooked, about 10 minutes. Add potatoes and continue cooking until vegetables are done, about 10 minutes longer. Fry bacon in a skillet, drain and add. Simmer 2 minutes more. Place slices of French bread in each plate and pour the soup over them.

Serves 6-8.

POTAGE CRÈME À LA NIVERNAISE

Cream of Carrot Soup

4 tablespoons butter
5 carrots, peeled and thinly sliced
1 teaspoon sugar
1 teaspoon salt
4 tablespoons water
2 tablespoons flour
¼ teaspoon freshly ground white pepper
2½ cups milk
½ cup cream

Melt 2 tablespoons butter in a heavy saucepan, add the carrots, sugar, ½ teaspoon salt, and the water. Cover and cook over low heat for 20 minutes.

Melt remaining butter in a saucepan and blend in flour, the remaining ½ teaspoon salt, and the pepper. Gradually add the milk, stirring to the boiling point. Cook a few minutes, stirring continually. Dice a few cooked carrot slices and set aside. Mix the rest into the sauce and cook for 45 minutes in the top of a double boiler. Purée in an electric blender or force through a fine sieve. Mix in the cream and reserved diced carrots, reheat and serve.

Serves 4.

SOUPE AU PISTOU

Bean and Pasta Soup

2½ quarts water
2 pounds potatoes, peeled
2 pounds fresh lima beans, shelled or 1 package frozen, thawed
3 large ripe tomatoes, skinned, seeded, and chopped
1 pound vermicelli or other small pasta
Salt, freshly ground black pepper
5 cloves garlic, chopped
12 fresh basil leaves or 1 teaspoon dried
2 tablespoons olive oil
1 cup grated Parmesan cheese

Put in a large saucepan the water, potatoes, beans, and tomatoes. Bring to a boil, reduce heat, and simmer 30 minutes, or until vegetables are cooked. Stir in vermicelli and simmer 10 minutes very gently until tender, stirring frequently. Season with salt and pepper to taste. Pound the garlic, basil, and olive oil to a paste. Mix well, stir paste into soup, and cook 1 minute. Stir in grated cheese and serve.

Serves 8.

BOUILLABAISSE MARSEILLAISE

Fish Soup, Marseille Style

⅓ cup olive oil
1½ cups chopped onions
2 cloves garlic, minced
2 cups chopped fresh tomatoes or drained canned tomatoes
1 cup dry white wine
3 cups bottled clam juice
1 bay leaf
½ teaspoon thyme
⅛ teaspoon crushed fennel seeds
⅛ teaspoon saffron
2 pounds assorted fish, cut in serving-sized pieces
1 1½-pound lobster cut up in the shell
¾ pound raw shrimp, shelled and deveined
½ pound scallops
12 mussels or clams or both, scrubbed
2 tablespoons chopped parsley

Heat the oil in a large kettle; sauté the onions and garlic 5 minutes. Add the tomatoes, wine, clam juice, bay leaf, thyme, fennel, and saffron. Bring to a boil and cook over low heat 30 minutes. Add the fish and seafood. Cook 20 minutes longer. Stir in the parsley, remove bay leaf. Serve in deep plates with garlic-rubbed French bread toast.

Serves 6.

LA POCHOUSE BOURGUIGNONNE

Fish Chowder

4½ pounds mixed fresh-water fish (trout, pike, carp, eel, etc.)
6 tablespoons butter
2 tablespoons diced bacon
2 bottles dry white wine
Bouquet garni (or 1 bay leaf, sprig parsley, sprig thyme, tied together)
2 cloves garlic, halved
1 teaspoon meat glaze
2 tablespoons butter blended with 4 tablespoons flour
Salt, freshly ground pepper
½ cup warmed brandy
Slices of French bread, fried in butter and rubbed with garlic

Four or more types of fish are needed for this dish. After fish are cleaned and heads and tails removed, you should have 4½ pounds. Cut fish into pieces 1½ inches thick. Melt the 6 tablespoons butter in a deep saucepan, add the bacon, and sauté until golden. Add the wine, bouquet garni, garlic, and bring to a boil. Reduce heat and simmer 20 minutes. Add fish and cook 20 minutes over medium heat. Blend in the meat glaze and butter-flour mixture (*beurre manié*). Taste for seasoning and add salt and pepper if necessary. Set brandy aflame and add, shaking pan till flames die down.

Put French bread in bottom of a deep tureen and pour soup over it. Serve at once.

Serves 6-8.

Eggs, Cheese and Bread

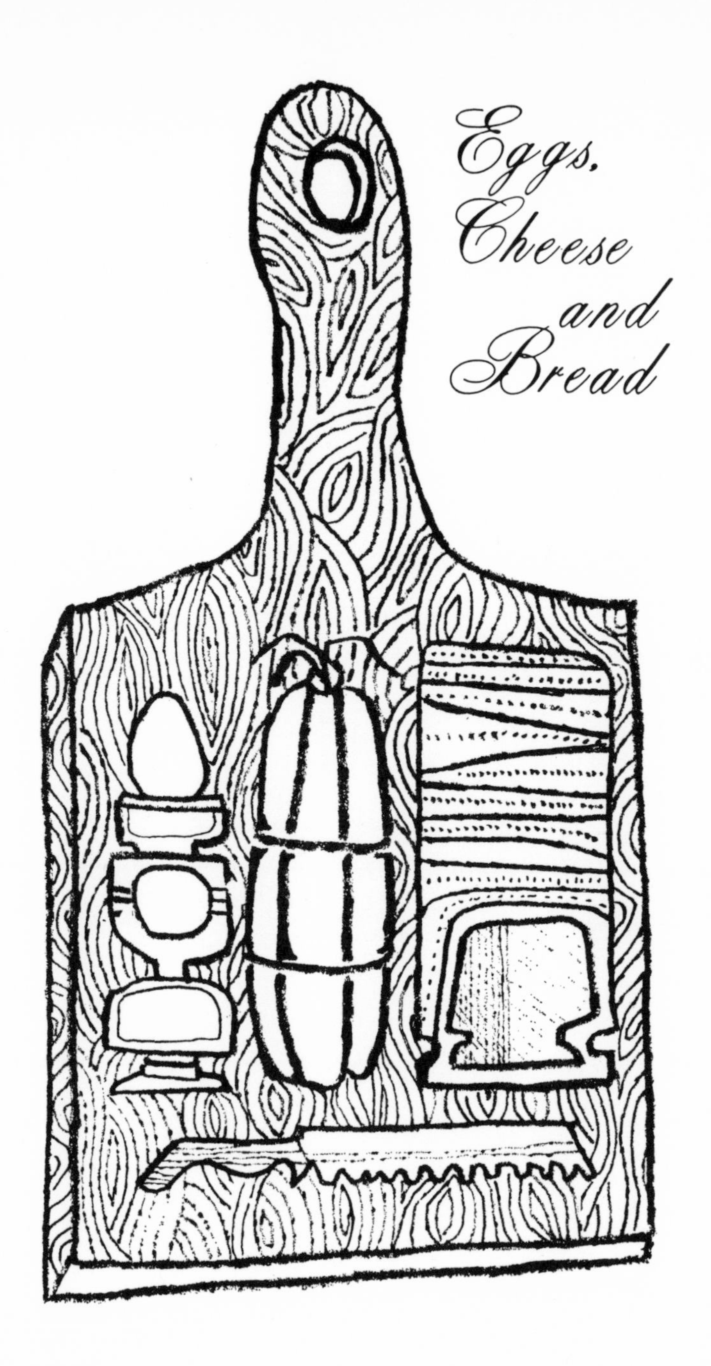

Eggs, Cheese and Bread

OMELETTE BAYONNAISE

Ham Omelet

2 tablespoons butter
¼ pound mushrooms, sliced
½ cup diced cooked ham
1 tablespoon sour cream
A few tarragon leaves, chopped, or ¼ teaspoon dried
4 eggs
½ teaspoon salt
¼ teaspoon freshly ground black pepper

Melt 1 tablespoon butter in a skillet and lightly sauté the mushrooms and ham. Mix in the sour cream and tarragon. Heat through. Set aside while preparing the omelet.

Beat the eggs in a bowl with 2 tablespoons cold water and salt and pepper until well blended but not too foamy. Heat an omelet pan until very hot, melt remaining butter, and pour in eggs. Make the omelet, leaving the center moist and creamy. Fill with the mushroom mixture, fold over, and serve at once.

Serves 2.

OMELETTE MOUSSELINE

Fluffy Omelet

3 egg yolks
¼ teaspoon salt
1 tablespoon heavy cream
3 egg whites, stiffly beaten
2 tablespoons butter

Beat together the egg yolks, salt and cream. Fold in the egg whites. Melt the butter in a 9-inch skillet until it sizzles; pour the egg mixture into it. Cook over medium heat, until set, shaking the pan almost constantly to bring the edges into the center. Roll up and turn out onto a heated dish.

Serves 2.

LA PIPÉRADE

Pepper Omelet

2 tablespoons olive oil
1 small green pepper, finely sliced
1 small onion, chopped
1 clove garlic, chopped and mashed
2 ripe tomatoes, skinned, seeded, and coarsely chopped
Salt, freshly ground black pepper
1 tablespoon shredded cooked ham
1 tablespoon butter
4 eggs

Heat the oil in a skillet and sauté the green pepper very slowly for 3 minutes. Add the onion, garlic, tomatoes, salt and pepper to taste, and the ham and simmer slowly about 30 minutes or until vegetables are soft. Add butter.

Beat eggs slightly with salt and pepper and mix them vigorously into the vegetables, raising the heat so the eggs cook quickly. Slide whole omelet onto a hot platter and serve.

Serves 2.

OMELETTE À LA SAVOYARDE

Potato and Cheese Omelet

½ cup julienne-cut potatoes
4 tablespoons butter
4 eggs
2 tablespoons heavy cream
1 teaspoon salt
⅛ teaspoon freshly ground white pepper
¼ cup julienne-cut Swiss or Gruyère cheese

Sauté the potatoes in 2 tablespoons butter until golden brown. Cool slightly. Beat the eggs, cream, salt and pepper, and mix in the potatoes and cheese. Heat the remaining butter in a 9-inch skillet and pour in the egg mixture. Cook, stirring the edges into the center, until set. Turn out, without folding, onto a hot serving dish.

Serves 2.

OMELETTE AUX TRUFFES

Truffle Omelet

4 eggs
Salt, freshly ground black pepper
1 truffle, sliced
1 tablespoon Madeira
2 tablespoons butter

Season eggs with salt and pepper and beat with a fork for 30 seconds. Add truffle slices, reserving a few, and Madeira. Heat an omelet pan. Add the butter. When melted, pour in egg mixture and make omelet. Eggs should be cooked but still creamy on top. Fold omelet, turn out onto a hot dish, and top with reserved truffle slices.

Serves 2.

OMELETTE PROVENÇALE

Herb Omelet

2 tablespoons oil
2 tomatoes, skinned, seeded, and finely chopped
1 clove garlic, finely chopped
1 very small onion, finely chopped
6 sprigs parsley, chopped
4 sprigs fresh tarragon, chopped
Salt, freshly ground black pepper
4 eggs
1 tablespoon butter

Heat the oil in a skillet. Add the tomatoes, garlic, onion, parsley, tarragon; season with salt and pepper, and sauté 10 minutes.

Beat eggs with a fork for 30 seconds and season with a little salt and pepper. Heat omelet pan and add butter. When melted, pour in egg mixture and quickly cook omelet. It should not be dry. While eggs are still soft, spread sautéed vegetable mixture in center. Fold over, turn out onto a hot platter, and serve immediately.

Serves 2.

OEUFS À LA BOURGUIGNONNE

Poached Eggs, Burgundy Style

10 slices of bacon, diced
3 tablespoons butter
½ cup chopped onions
2 tablespoons flour
1¼ teaspoons salt
¼ teaspoon freshly ground black pepper
⅛ teaspoon garlic powder
1 cup beef stock
1 cup dry red wine
⅛ teaspoon thyme
1 bay leaf
2 tablespoons minced parsley
8 eggs
French bread or toast

Fry the bacon until crisp in a saucepan. Remove. Pour off fat. Add butter to pan, melt, add onions and sauté until lightly browned. Stir in the flour, salt, pepper, and garlic powder. Slowly add the stock and wine, stirring to the boiling point. Add the thyme, bay leaf, and parsley. Cook over low heat 20 minutes. Strain into a skillet, bring to a boil. Poach the eggs, two at a time, in the sauce. Serve each egg on a slice of sautéed or toasted French bread and pour the sauce over the top.

Serves 4-8.

OEUFS EN MATELOTE

Eggs in Red Wine

1 onion, thinly sliced
1 clove garlic
1½ cups water
1½ cups dry red wine
½ teaspoon salt
¼ teaspoon freshly ground black pepper
Bouquet garni (or 4 sprigs parsley, sprig of thyme, bay leaf, tied together)
8 eggs
1 tablespoon flour
2 tablespoons butter
Large croutons of fried bread

Combine the onion, garlic, water, wine, salt, pepper, and herbs in a deep skillet. Bring to a boil and simmer 15 minutes. Remove the onion, garlic, and herbs. Poach the eggs in the liquid. When the whites are thoroughly set (about 5 minutes), remove eggs and drain. Place on a heated serving dish and keep warm. Increase the heat and reduce the liquid by half. Mix the flour and butter together and form into tiny balls. Gradually drop them into the hot liquid and simmer for a few minutes, or until liquid is thickened. Do not boil. Pour sauce over the eggs and serve with croutons.

Serves 4.

FONDUE JURASSIENNE

Hot Cheese Dip

2 cloves garlic, chopped
1½ cups dry white wine
¾ pound Gruyère cheese, cut in slivers
⅓ cup milk
Salt, freshly ground white pepper
1½ tablespoons kirsch (clear cherry liqueur)
2 tablespoons sweet butter
French bread or toast

Put the garlic and wine in an earthenware casserole and cook until the wine is reduced a little. Strain wine and reserve.

Put the cheese and milk in the casserole and cook over low heat, stirring continuously, until cheese is melted and mixture smooth and creamy. Season with a little salt and pepper and mix in the wine and the kirsch. Stir in the butter and serve at once with pieces of crusty French bread or toast.

Serves 4-6.

GOUGÈRE BOURGUIGNONNE

Cheese Puff Ring

¾ cup water
½ teaspoon salt
4 tablespoons butter
1½ cups sifted flour
3 eggs
1 cup cubed Swiss or Gruyère cheese

Put the water, salt, and butter in a saucepan. Bring to a boil and dump in the flour, all at once. Stir constantly over low heat until dough forms a ball and comes away from the sides of the pan. Remove from heat. Let cool 5 minutes. Beat in the eggs, one at a time, mixing until smooth after each egg is added. Mix in the cheese. Form into a ring on a baking sheet.

Meanwhile, preheat oven to 425°. Bake until browned, about 25 minutes. Do not open oven door during baking or gougère will fall. Serve hot or cold.

Tablespoons of the mixture may be baked and served as hot appetizers in the same manner as cocktail puffs. In this case, bake the puffs for 12 minutes only.

Serves 4-6.

BRIOCHE

Yeast Bread

1 envelope yeast
2 tablespoons sugar
½ cup lukewarm water
5 cups sifted flour
½ teaspoon salt
¾ pound butter
8 eggs
½ cup milk, scalded and cooled
Beaten egg yolk

Dissolve the yeast and 1 tablespoon sugar in the water. Stir in 1 cup flour and mix to a soft ball. Cut top criss-cross with a knife. Cover and let stand in a warm place until double in bulk.

Sift 2 cups flour into a bowl with the salt. Work in half the butter, 2 eggs, and the remaining sugar. Mix in the milk. Beat in the remaining butter, 2 eggs, and the remaining flour. Knead, picking dough up and slapping it down until smooth and not sticky. Work in the yeast mixture and the remaining eggs. Knead until very smooth, glossy, and elastic. Place in a greased bowl, cover with a towel, and let stand in a warm place until double in bulk, about 2½ hours. Punch down, cover, and refrigerate overnight.

Brioche may be baked in individual brioche molds or cup-cake tins, or in 2 large brioche molds. In either case, form balls of dough large enough to half-fill the molds. Cut a cross in the top and press into it a small ball of dough which will form the top or crown. Cover and set to rise in a warm place until double in bulk, about 45 minutes. Brush tops with beaten egg yolk. Bake in a preheated 425° oven, allowing 20 minutes for small brioche, 50 minutes for large, or until browned. Makes about 18 small, 2 large brioches.

Serve for breakfast with coffee.

CROISSANTS

Breakfast Crescents

2 envelopes or cakes yeast
¼ cup lukewarm water
1 tablespoon sugar
4 cups sifted flour
½ teaspoon salt
½ cup scalded milk, cooled
¾ pound butter
Beaten egg

Dissolve the yeast in the water with the sugar. Stir in 1 cup flour until a ball forms. Cut top criss-cross with a knife, cover, and let stand in a warm place until double in bulk.

Sift the remaining flour and the salt into a bowl. Stir in the milk, then beat in the yeast mixture. Cover and let stand 15 minutes.

Roll out the dough into a long rectangle on a lightly floured board. Work butter with the hands into a flat cake and place in center of dogh. Fold over one side, then the other, making three layers. Turn open ends toward you and roll out. Fold over in thirds again (this is called a turn). Repeat twice more, making three turns in all. Wrap in a towel and chill overnight.

Roll out the dough in the manner described three times. Chill 1 hour. Roll out dough ⅛ inch thick and cut into 6-inch squares. Cut each square into 2 triangles. Roll up from long end into a cylinder. Arrange on a baking sheet, turning ends in to form crescents. Cover and let rise in a warm place until double in bulk, about 1 hour.

Brush tops with beaten egg and bake in a preheated 425° oven 5 minutes. Reduce heat to 350° and bake 15 minutes longer, or until brown. Makes about 24.

Serve for breakfast with coffee.

Fish

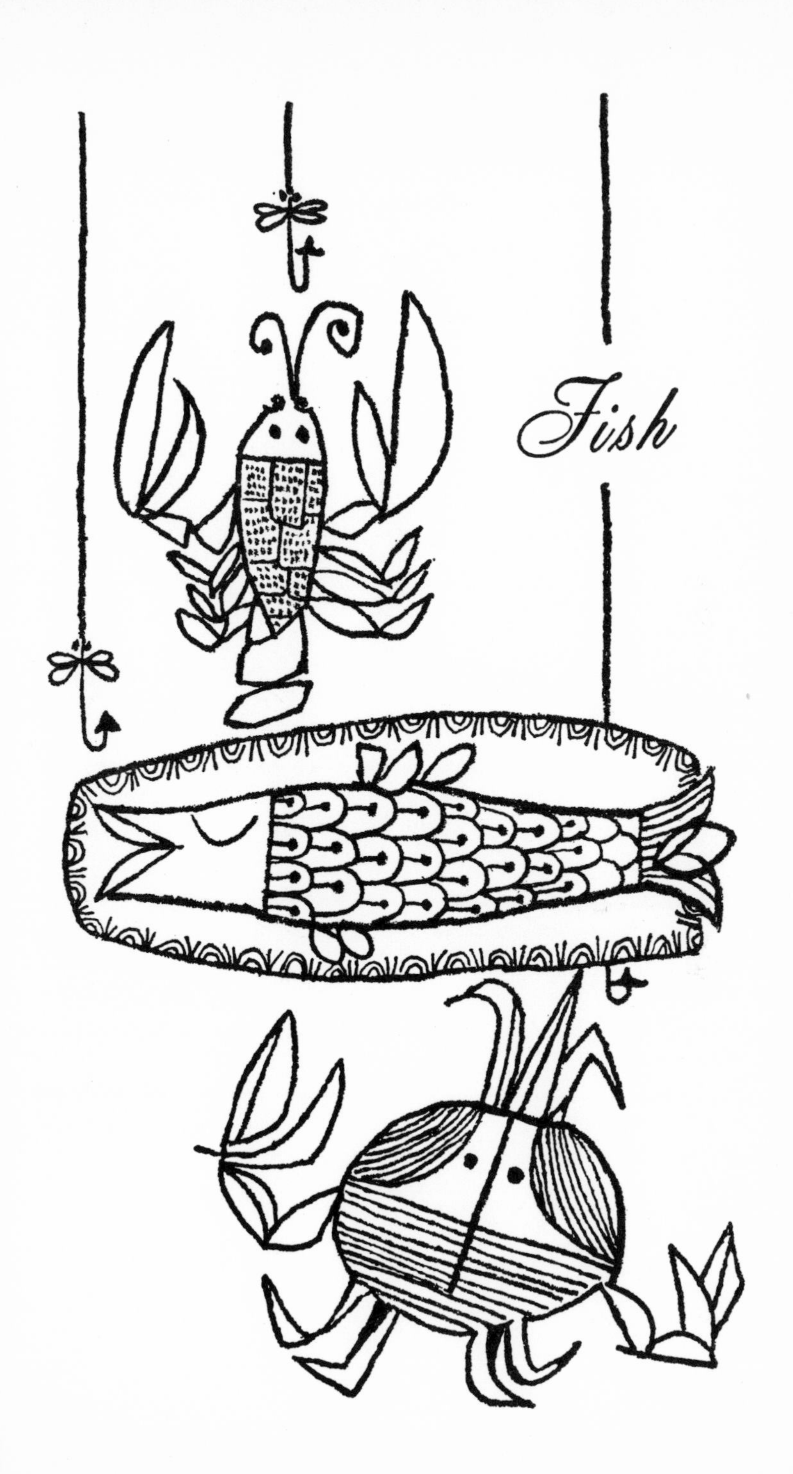

Fish

CREVETTES À LA CRÈME

Creamed Shrimp

2 tablespoons butter
1½ pounds raw shrimp, shelled and deveined
Salt, freshly ground black pepper
2 tablespoons warmed brandy
2 tablespoons tomato paste
3 shallots, finely chopped
1 tablespoon chopped parsley
1 bay leaf
Pinch of thyme
1 cup dry white wine
5 tablespoons heavy cream

Melt the butter in a saucepan and sauté the shrimp for a few minutes, turning once or twice. Season to taste with salt and pepper. Set 1 tablespoon brandy afire and pour over shrimp. Stir in tomato paste, shallots, parsley, bay leaf, thyme, and wine. Cook 8 minutes. Stir in the cream. Remove shrimp, strain sauce, and reduce it a little, if necessary. Mix in remaining brandy, pour sauce over shrimp, and serve.

Serves 4.

CREVETTES À LA BORDELAISE

Shrimp in White Wine

2 pounds raw shrimp
¼ pound butter
1 cup chopped onions
1 cup grated carrots
2 tablespoons minced parsley
1 bay leaf
⅛ teaspoon thyme
1 teaspoon salt
½ teaspoon freshly ground black pepper
¼ cup brandy
1 tablespoon tomato paste
1½ cups dry white wine

Shell and devein shrimp. Melt half the butter in a skillet and in it sauté the vegetables and parsley for 10 minutes. Add bay leaf, thyme, shrimp. Season with salt and pepper. Sauté 2 minutes. Slightly warm the brandy, pour over shrimp mixture, and flame. When flames have died, remove shrimp, and stir in tomato paste and wine, blending well. Cook 5 minutes over medium heat. Strain sauce through a sieve or food mill, pressing to purée vegetables. Return sauce to skillet with shrimp and cook 5 minutes only, over low heat. Add remaining butter, bit by bit, and cook just until melted. Taste for seasoning.

Serves 4-6.

COQUILLES SAINT-JACQUES

Creamed Scallops

1 pound scallops
1½ cups water
¾ cup dry white wine
2 sprigs parsley
1 bay leaf
½ pound mushrooms, chopped
1 cup finely chopped onions
2 tablespoons sherry
1 teaspoon lemon juice
6 tablespoons butter
3 tablespoons flour
2 egg yolks
4 tablespoons heavy cream
1¼ teaspoons salt
¼ teaspoon freshly ground white pepper
½ cup dry bread crumbs

Combine the scallops, 1½ cups water, wine, parsley, and bay leaf in a saucepan and bring to a boil. Reduce heat to a simmer and cook 5 minutes, or until tender. Discard the parsley and bay leaf; drain scallops, reserving liquid. Combine the mushrooms in a saucepan with the onions, sherry, lemon juice, and 2 tablespoons butter. Cover and cook 10 minutes. Strain and reserve the liquid.

Melt 3 tablespoons butter in a saucepan and blend in the flour. Add the liquids reserved from the scallops and mushroom-onion mixture, stirring to the boiling point. Simmer 3 minutes or until thickened. Beat the egg yolks and cream in a bowl and mix in a little of the hot sauce, stirring steadily to prevent curdling. Return to pan and cook until thickened; do not allow to boil. Season with the salt and pepper. Cut scallops in small pieces and add to sauce with the mushroom-onion mixture. Mix well and spoon into 6 scallop shells or ramekins. Cover with the bread crumbs, dot with remaining butter. Bake in a 425° oven 10 minutes. Garnish with parsley sprigs.

Serves 6.

HOMARD À L'ARMORICAINE

Lobster Armorican

1 live lobster (about 2 pounds)
2 tablespoons butter
1 tablespoon oil
1 small onion, chopped
1 clove garlic, chopped and mashed
Bouquet garni (or 1 bay leaf, sprig parsley, and piece celery, tied together)
1 tomato, skinned, seeded, and coarsely chopped
1 tablespoon warmed brandy
1 cup dry white wine
1 teaspoon salt
½ teaspoon white pepper
1 tablespoon flour
1 teaspoon lemon juice
1 tablespoon heavy cream
Chopped parsley

Split the live lobster in half lengthwise. Remove and reserve the coral. Remove and discard the intestinal vein and sac behind the eyes. Heat 1 tablespoon butter and the oil in a heavy pan and lightly sauté the lobster until the shell turns red. Remove from pan. Add to the pan the onion, garlic, bouquet garni, and tomato and simmer 2 minutes. Replace lobster; set brandy aflame and pour over lobster. Add the wine, cover pan, and simmer 30 minutes. Season with salt and pepper.

Remove lobster to a hot serving dish. Mash the reserved coral to a paste with the remaining butter and the flour and blend into the pan juices. Add lemon juice and heavy cream, and adjust seasoning. Strain sauce over the lobster and sprinkle with chopped parsley. Serve with rice.

Serves 2.

QUENELLES DE BROCHET

Fish Mousse Balls

BATTER

1 cup water
1 teaspoon salt
4 tablespoons butter
1 cup sifted flour
2 eggs

Bring the water, salt, and butter to a boil. When butter melts, remove saucepan from the heat and beat in the flour all at once with a wooden spoon. Return to the heat and cook, beating steadily until mixture forms a ball and leaves the sides of the pan. Remove from the heat and beat in 1 egg at a time, then beat until smooth and glossy. Put in a mixing bowl.

FISH MIXTURE

1½ pounds boneless pike or halibut
1¼ teaspoons salt
½ teaspoon white pepper
⅛ teaspoon nutmeg
¼ cup heavy cream
1 cup clam juice
3 cups water

Grind the fish three times in a meat chopper or purée in an electric blender. Add to the batter with the salt, pepper, and nutmeg. Beat with an electric mixer or wooden spoon until very smooth and light. Taste for seasoning. Chill 2 hours. Beat in the cream very gradually.

Bring the clam juice and water to a boil in a large skillet, then reduce heat to low. Use two wet round soup spoons to shape the quenelles. Pick up a spoon of the mixture and smooth the top with the other spoon. Carefully drop it into the skillet. Dip spoons in cold water and work quickly to shape remaining quenelles. Don't crowd skillet, as they double in size. Cook over low heat 20 minutes. Remove with a slotted spoon and drain well. Serve with *Sauce Nantua* (Seafood Sauce) (see recipe).

Serves 4.

FILETS DE MAQUEREAUX

Sautéed Mackerel Fillets

3 tablespoons butter
½ cup chopped onions
1 cup chopped mushrooms
1 clove garlic, minced
1 tablespoon wine vinegar
3 teaspoons salt
¾ teaspoon freshly ground black pepper
4 fillets of mackerel
¾ cup flour
½ cup salad oil
2 tablespoons minced parsley

Melt the butter in a skillet and sauté the onions, mushrooms, and garlic until browned. Mix in the vinegar, 1 teaspoon salt, and ¼ teaspoon pepper. Keep warm.

Season the fillets with the remaining salt and pepper and roll in the flour. Heat the oil in a skillet and sauté the fish on both sides until browned. Remove to a serving platter and cover with the vegetables. Sprinkle with the parsley. Serve with sautéed tomatoes.

Serves 4.

MAQUEREAU À LA FLAMANDE

Stuffed Mackerel, Family Style

2- to 3-pound mackerel
2 teaspoons salt
¾ teaspoon freshly ground black pepper
4 tablespoons softened butter
4 tablespoons chopped onion
2 tablespoons chopped parsley
1 tablespoon chopped chives
2 teaspoons lemon juice

Have the fish split for stuffing, and boned. The head and tail may be left on, or not, as you prefer. Season the fish with 1½ teaspoons salt and ½ teaspoon pepper. Blend the softened butter with the onion, parsley, chives, 1 teaspoon lemon juice, and the remaining salt and pepper. Blend well together. Stuff the fish with this mixture. Wrap the fish in oiled waxed paper or aluminum foil and tie at both ends. Bake in a 350° oven 45 minutes. Transfer fish to a hot serving platter and unwrap very carefully. Pour the butter and juices from the wrapping and the remaining lemon juice over the fish. Garnish with parsley.

Serves 4.

DARNE DE SAUMON À LA MONTPELLIER

Salmon in Green Butter

2 cups water
1 cup dry white wine
1 onion, sliced
½ carrot, sliced
3 whole peppercorns, crushed
1½ teaspoons salt
Bouquet garni (or bay leaf, 1 sprig parsley, 1 sprig thyme, and celery stalk with leaves, tied together)
2½-pound center cut salmon

Combine the water, wine, onion, carrot, peppercorns, salt, and bouquet garni in a deep saucepan. Bring to a boil, reduce heat, and simmer 20 minutes. Cool 10 minutes. Wrap salmon in cheesecloth, tie securely, and lower gently into court-bouillon. Simmer over low heat 30 minutes or until done. Cool in liquid, remove carefully, and skin. Pat dry, chill, and spread top and sides with the green butter. Arrange on a platter and surround with parsley.

GREEN BUTTER

1 bunch water cress
4 sprigs parsley
5 lettuce leaves
Handful of spinach leaves
Leaves from 1 stalk celery
2 quarts water
1 small sour pickle, finely chopped
12 capers, finely chopped
4 anchovy fillets, finely chopped
1 clove garlic, finely chopped
½ pound sweet butter
1 teaspoon dried tarragon leaves
1 teaspoon dried basil leaves
½ teaspoon Dijon-style mustard
Salt, freshly ground black pepper
Lemon juice

Wash water cress, parsley, lettuce, spinach, and celery leaves, and remove heavy stems. Bring water to a boil in a deepp pan, remove from heat, and add the washed greens. Cover pan tightly and allow greens to stand 3 minutes. Drain well. Place greens in a towel and squeeze out remaining water. Purée the greens in an electric blender, or chop and force through a fine sieve.

Chop the pickle, capers, anchovy fillets, and garlic until very smooth. Cream butter until very light and fluffy and add the two puréed mixtures, the tarragon, basil, mustard, a little salt and pepper, and a few drops lemon juice. Mix only enough to blend throughly. Spread this green butter over the salmon.

Serves 4-5.

ALOSE À LA PROVENÇALE

Shad Provençal

2 pounds sorrel or spinach or 2 packages frozen spinach, thawed
2 tablespoons olive oil
¾ cup chopped onions
1 cup peeled, chopped tomatoes
1 clove garlic, minced
2½ teaspoons salt
½ teaspoon freshly ground black pepper
2 tablespoons dry bread crumbs
3 pounds shad, boned
3 tablespoons butter

Wash the sorrel or spinach, drain well, and shred. If frozen spinach is used, drain it thoroughly. Heat the oil in a skillet; sauté the onions 5 minutes. Mix in the sorrel or spinach, tomatoes, garlic, 1 teaspoon salt, and ¼ teaspoon pepper. Cook over low heat 10 minutes. Stir in the bread crumbs and taste for seasoning.

Season the shad with the remaining salt and pepper. Melt the butter in a skillet; brown the shad in it on both sides. Spread half the vegetable mixture on the bottom of a buttered baking dish. Arrange the shad over it and cover with the remaining vegetable mixture. Bake in a 325° oven 45

Serves 6.

minutes.

SOLES AU VIN BLANC

Sole in White Wine

4 fillets of sole
4 tablespoons butter
1 tablespoon chopped shallots
3 tablespoons chopped parsley
2 teaspoons salt
½ teaspoon freshly ground black pepper
½ cup dry white wine
½ cup dry bread crumbs

Wash the fillets and pat dry with paper towels.

Spread 1½ tablespoons butter, ½ tablespoon shallots, and 1½ tablespoons parsley on the bottom of a large shallow baking dish. Arrange the fillets on top and cover with 2 tablespoons butter, remaining shallots, and parsley. Season with the salt and pepper. Pour the wine over the fish, cover with the bread crumbs, and dot with the remaining butter. Bake in a 350° oven 35 minutes. Serve in the baking dish, garnished with parsley.

Serves 4.

SOLE NORMANDE

Sole with Shrimp Sauce

12 mussels, well scrubbed
¼ cup white wine
¼ pound mushrooms, sliced
1 tablespoon lemon juice
Salt, freshly ground black pepper
4 fillets of sole
12 cooked peeled shrimp
3 egg yolks
4 tablespoons softened butter

Cook the mussels gently in the wine until the shells open. Discard any that do not open. Half cover the mushrooms with water, add the lemon juice and a pinch of salt, and cook for 3 minutes. Strain liquid from mussels and mushrooms into a baking dish and add the sole. Season with salt and a little pepper and bake in a 300° oven 20 minutes. Transfer to a hot serving platter, and surround with the mussels, mushrooms, and the cooked shrimp. Keep warm. Strain the cooking liquid and reduce to about ¼ cup by rapid boiling. Put egg yolks in top of double boiler and beat well over very gentle heat, stirring in softened butter. Add reduced liquid, beating constantly with a whisk. When sauce is thick and foamy, pour over the sole.

Serves 4.

SOLE À LA BOURGUIGNONNE

Sole in Red Wine

2 cups thinly sliced onions
6 tablespoons butter
¼ pound mushrooms, sliced
4 fillets of sole
1½ teaspoons salt
½ teaspoon freshly ground black pepper
½ cup dry red wine
1 tablespoon flour

Sauté the onions in a skillet in 2 tablespoons butter until golden. Remove. Add 2 tablespoons butter and the mushrooms. Sauté 3 minutes. Spread onions on a baking dish and arrange the fillets and mushrooms on top. Season with salt and pepper and pour on all but 2 tablespoons of the wine. Bake 25 minutes in a 375° oven or until fish flakes easily. Remove fish to hot serving dish. Mix the flour and the reserved wine and stir into the pan juices. Cook over medium heat, stirring, until thickened. Add the rest of the butter. Adjust seasoning. Pour sauce over fish and, if desired, glaze for a minute under a hot broiler.

Serves 4.

TRUITE AMANDINE

Trout with Almonds

6 brook trout
¾ cup flour
1 tablespoon salt
½ teaspoon freshly ground black pepper
1 cup milk
½ cup salad oil
6 tablespoons butter
¾ cup sliced blanched almonds

Wash trout and dry well. Season the flour with the salt and pepper. Dip trout in milk, then in seasoned flour. Heat oil in a skillet and sauté trout until they are browned all over and the flesh flakes easily. Remove to a hot serving platter and keep warm. Pour off oil. Melt butter in skillet and sauté almonds until brown. Scatter over the fish.

Serves 6.

GRENOUILLES À LA POULETTE

Frogs' Legs in White Wine

12 pairs frogs' legs
2 tablespoons butter
2 tablespoons flour
½ cup dry white wine
2 tablespoons chopped onion
2 tablespoons chopped parsley
1¼ teaspoons salt
¼ teaspoon freshly ground black pepper
1 egg yolk
2 tablespoons heavy cream

Wash the frogs' legs, place in cold water, and soak 3 hours. Drain. Dry thoroughly on paper towels.

Melt the butter in a heavy saucepan and sauté the frogs' legs 2 minutes on each side. Stir the flour into the butter until well blended. Slowly add the wine, stirring constantly; mix in the onion and parsley and season with the salt and pepper. Cook over medium heat 15 minutes. Transfer frogs' legs to a hot serving dish. Beat the egg yolk with the cream and stir in a little of the hot sauce, mixing steadily to prevent curdling. Return to pan, still stirring continuously; heat but do not boil, and pour over the frogs' legs. Serve immediately.

Serves 4.

Poultry

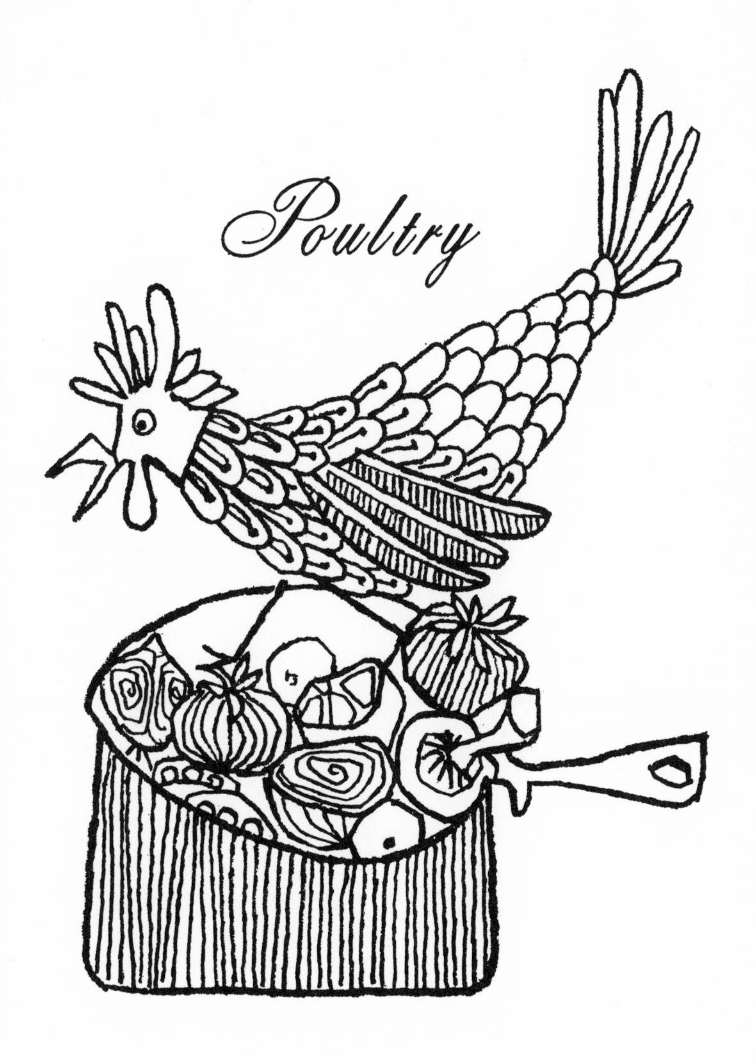

Poultry

POULET BASQUAIS

CHICKEN, BASQUE STYLE

3 tablespoons olive oil
3 tablespoons butter
1 3½-pound chicken
Salt, freshly ground black pepper
2 tablespoons warmed brandy
1 green pepper, diced
1 red pepper, diced
1 large tomato, skinned, seeded, and diced
1 small onion, chopped
1 clove garlic, chopped
1 shallot, chopped
2 tablespoons diced cooked ham

Heat 2 tablespoons oil and 2 tablespoons butter in a heavy Dutch oven or casserole. Brown the whole chicken slowly on all sides. Season to taste with salt and pepper and cook in a 350° oven until tender, about 1 hour. Set brandy afire and pour over chicken. Cut into serving pieces and keep warm.

Heat remaining butter and oil in another saucepan and cook diced red and green peppers until almost soft. Add tomato, onion, garlic, shallot, ham, and salt and pepper to taste, and continue cooking a further 5 minutes. Arrange chicken with juices on a hot serving platter, cover with the pepper sauce, and serve with fluffy boiled rice. If desired, cover the chicken parts with small pieces of spicy, fried sausages.

Serves 4.

POULET À LA NIÇOISE

Chicken, Nice Style

1 5-pound roasting chicken, disjointed
1 tablespoon salt
½ teaspoon freshly ground black pepper
3 tablespoons olive oil
2 tablespoons butter
1 teaspoon saffron
3 cloves garlic, minced
2 bay leaves
¼ teaspoon thyme
¼ teaspoon tarragon
4 tomatoes, quartered
1 cup dry white wine
1 cup canned chicken broth
½ cup pitted green olives
½ cup pitted black olives

Rub the chicken with the salt and pepper. Heat the olive oil and butter in a casserole; brown the chicken in it. Blend in the saffron and add the garlic, bay leaves, thyme, tarragon, tomatoes, wine, and broth. Cover and cook over low heat 1 hour or until chicken is tender. Add the olives, taste for seasoning, and cook 10 minutes longer. Discard bay leaves.

Serves 4-5.

POULET RÔTI

Roast Chicken

1 4-pound roasting chicken
2½ teaspoons salt
½ teaspoon freshly ground black pepper
1 clove garlic, minced
1 teaspoon paprika
3 tablespoons butter
½ cup chicken stock

Clean the chicken and wash inside and out. Dry well with paper towels. Combine the salt, pepper, garlic, and paprika, and rub the chicken all over with it. Truss. Put chicken on a rack in a shallow roasting pan, on its side. Spread with 2 tablespoons of the butter, softened. Pour ¼ cup water in the bottom of the pan and roast the chicken in a 425° oven for 15 minutes. Reduce heat to 350° and continue roasting for 1¼ minutes. Reduce heat to 350° and continue roasting for 1¼ hours, or until tender. Baste and turn frequently and add about ¼ cup more water to the pan, if necessary. Roast chicken breast upward for the last 15 minutes. Remove chicken to a platter. Mix the stock into the pan juices and cook over medium heat 3 minutes, scraping up glaze from bottom of pan. Add remaining butter, season to taste. Serve with chicken.

Serves 4.

POULET SAINTE-MENEHOULD

Crusted Broiled Chicken

1 2½-pound broiler, split
Salt, freshly ground black pepper
4 tablespoons olive oil
2 eggs, beaten
1 cup dry bread crumbs
¼ cup melted butter
Water cress

Sprinkle the chicken with salt and pepper and rub each side with oil. Broil, not too close to the flame, 10 minutes on each side. Remove and brush insides with beaten egg. Sprinkle with bread crumbs, coat with melted butter, and sprinkle again with bread crumbs. Broil 3 minutes longer or until crumbs are browned. Remove. Repeat egg, bread crumbs, and butter coating on top side of chicken and broil 3 minutes. Transfer to hot platter and garnish with water cress.

Serves 2-4.

POULET SAUTÉ À LA BORDELAISE

Chicken, Bordeaux Style

1 4- to 5-pound roasting chicken, disjointed
¼ pound butter
2 tablespoons olive oil
Salt, freshly ground black pepper
3 small artichokes
3 medium potatoes, peeled and very thinly sliced
3 onions, thinly sliced
Milk
Flour
Oil for deep frying
8 sprigs parsley
1 clove garlic, chopped and mashed
½ cup chicken stock
½ cup dry white wine
1 teaspoon meat glaze
1 tablespoon tomato paste

Sauté the chicken in 3 tablespoons butter and the olive oil, turning the parts to brown all sides. Season with salt and pepper. Cover and cook 45 minutes, or until tender. Transfer to center of a hot serving platter and keep warm.

While chicken is cooking, cut tops from artichokes and boil in salted water 35 minutes. Cut in quarters, discard choke (center). Sauté quartered artichokes in 2 tablespoons butter, turning frequently. Dry potatoes thoroughly and sauté in the remaining butter until golden brown on both sides.

Separate onion slices into rings. Dip in milk and then in flour and fry in 375° oil until crisp and golden. Dry parsley thoroughly, drop in hot oil, fry 3 seconds, and remove. Drain on paper towels.

Add garlic to butter remaining in pan in which chicken was cooked. Sauté 2 minutes. Mix in stock, wine, and meat glaze, and stir to lift glaze from pan. Simmer until liquid is slightly reduced. Strain into small saucepan and blend in tomato paste. Reheat.

Arrange the artichoke quarters in parallel rows on each side of chicken. Put mounds of potatoes and onions at each end and tuck parsley between chicken pieces. Pour sauce over chicken and serve.

Serves 4-6.

COQ AU VIN DE BOURGOGNE

Chicken in Red Wine

1 4-pound roasting chicken, disjointed
2 tablespoons butter
12 small white onions
2 slices of lean bacon, diced
¼ cup warmed brandy
3 cups dry red wine
1 cup chicken stock
2 cloves garlic, chopped
1 bay leaf
Salt, freshly ground black pepper
8 mushroom caps
2 tablespoons butter blended with 1 tablespoon flour

Wash the chicken pieces and dry well. Melt the butter in a flameproof casserole; add the onions and bacon and sauté until onions are lightly browned. Remove onions and bacon. Add chicken to pan and sauté on all sides until a light golden color. Set brandy afire and pour over chicken. Add wine, stock, garlic, bay leaf, and season to taste with salt and pepper. Stir to the boiling point and add onions and bacon with mushrooms. Reduce heat, cover, and simmer for about 45 minutes, or until chicken is tender. Remove and discard bay leaf and skim excess fat from liquid. Thicken by stirring in the butter-flour mixture until dissolved. Serve in the casserole.

Serves 4.

POULET MARENGO

Chicken Marengo

1 4-pound roasting chicken, disjointed
3 tablespoons olive oil
2 tablespoons butter
1 teaspoon shallots, chopped
1 teaspoon salt
¼ teaspoon freshly ground pepper
1 cup dry white wine
1 tablespoon tomato paste
1 cup chicken stock
½ pound mushrooms, sautéed

Wash and dry the chicken pieces. Heat the oil and butter in a heatproof casserole or Dutch oven and sauté the chicken until browned all over. Add shallots, salt, pepper, and the wine. Cook until wine is reduced by half. Add tomato paste and chicken stock. Cover and cook over low heat 45 minutes or until tender.

Transfer chicken to a heated serving platter. Reduce sauce slightly. If too thin, thicken by stirring in 1 tablespoon butter blended with 1 tablespoon flour (*beurre manié*) and cook a few minutes more. Arrange cooked mushrooms on chicken, strain sauce over chicken, and serve hot.

Serves 4-6.

POULET AUX OLIVES

Chicken with Olives

1 4-pound roasting chicken
2½ teaspoons salt
½ teaspoon freshly ground white pepper
2 tablespoons butter
2 tablespoons flour
3 cups chicken stock
3 sprigs parsley
1 bay leaf
½ teaspoon rosemary
¾ cup pitted green olives

Clean and truss the chicken. Season with the salt and pepper. Melt butter in a large heavy pan and brown chicken all over. Remove. Mix in flour until browned. Add the stock, stirring to the boiling point. Add the parsley, bay leaf, rosemary, and return the chicken; cover and cook over low heat 1 hour or until tender. Add olives 15 minutes before end of cooking time. Place chicken on a hot serving platter, remove strings or skewers and bay leaf. Surround with olives and pour the sauce over the top. Serve with boiled potatoes or rice.

Serves 4-6.

POULET À L'ASTURIENNE

Stuffed Chicken, Asturian

½ pound chicken livers, diced
¼ pound butter
1 cup soft bread crumbs
¼ pound ham, cut julienne
4 pimientos, cut julienne
4 hard-cooked egg yolks, mashed
3 teaspoons salt
¾ teaspoon freshly ground black pepper
1½ teaspoons paprika
1 4-pound roasting chicken

Sauté the livers in half the butter for 5 minutes. Stir in the bread crumbs, ham, pimientos, egg yolks, 1 teaspoon salt, ¼ teaspoon pepper, and ½ teaspoon paprika. Season the chicken with the remaining salt, pepper, and paprika and stuff with the ham mixture. Close the openings with skewers or aluminum foil.

Melt the remaining butter in a casserole or Dutch oven. Place the chicken in it and cover and cook over low heat 1½ hours or until chicken is tender. Turn frequently and watch carefully to prevent burning. If necessary, add a little more butter. Serve with fried eggplant and broiled tomatoes.

Serves 4.

POULET À LA VALLÉE D'AUGE

Chicken with Apples and Cider

2 3-pound fryers, disjointed
2 teaspoons salt
½ teaspoon freshly ground black pepper
6 tablespoons butter
½ cup minced onions
2 apples, peeled and cut in eighths
4 tablespoons cognac or apple brandy
¾ cup cider
¼ teaspoon thyme
½ cup heavy cream

Season the chicken with the salt and pepper. Melt the butter in a casserole; brown the chicken in it. Add the onions and apples; cook 5 minutes. Warm the cognac, pour into the casserole, and set aflame. When flames die, add the cider and thyme. Cover and cook over low heat 30 minutes or until chicken is tender. Taste for seasoning.

Arrange the chicken on a heated platter. Stir the cream into the sauce, heat, but do not let boil. Pour over the chicken. Serve with fried apple rings.

Serves 8.

VOLAILLE AMANDINE

Chicken and Almonds

¾ cup thinly sliced onions
1 cup chopped green peppers
5 tablespoons butter
3 cups cubed cooked chicken
¼ teaspoon freshly ground white pepper
1 tablespoon flour
1 cup chicken stock
¼ pound mushrooms, sliced
1 cup blanched, sliced, toasted almonds

Sauté the onions and peppers in 4 tablespoons butter for 5 minutes, stirring frequently. Add chicken and sauté 5 minutes. Mix in the pepper and flour and slowly add the stock, stirring constantly. Cover and cook over low heat 20 minutes.

Melt remaining butter and sauté the mushrooms 5 minutes. Mix mushrooms and almonds with chicken and season to taste. Serve in hot patty shells or on toast.

Serves 6.

SUPRÊMES DE VOLAILLE STRASBOURGEOIS

Chicken Breasts with Pâté

2 chicken breasts, skinned, boned, and cut in half
3 tablespoons butter
1½ teaspoons salt
¼ teaspoon freshly ground white pepper
3 ounces canned pâté de foie gras
1 cup heavy cream

Sauté the chicken breasts in the hot butter for 20 minutes, or until tender, turning frequently. Season with the salt and pepper and place on a hot serving dish. Mash the *pâté* and cream and mix into the pan juices. Heat and pour over the chicken. Serve with noodles mixed with sautéed mushrooms.

Serves 4.

TERRINE DE VOLAILLE

Chicken in a Terrine

1 3½-pound chicken
½ pound ground fresh pork
½ pound ground veal
2 slices dry bread soaked in ¼ cup milk
2¼ teaspoons salt
¾ teaspoon freshly ground black pepper
½ pound veal cutlet, cut in thin strips
½ pound thin ham steak, cut in thin strips
2 paper-thin slices salt pork
1 bay leaf
½ teaspoon thyme
½ cup water
1 cup brandy

Clean the chicken. With a sharp boning knife, make an incision down the back and loosen the flesh from each side of the carcass, taking care not to pierce the skin. Remove all the bones but the leg and wing and spread out the chicken. (This is done to keep chicken in shape.)

Chop the liver and heart of the chicken fine and combine with the ground pork and veal. Drain the bread and add to tne meat mixture. Season with 1 teaspoon salt and ¼ teaspoon pepper and mix well together. Press the skin and flesh of the chicken as flat as possible (skin side down) and spread a layer of stuffing over it. Cover with a layer of the veal and ham strips. Continue alternating layers of stuffing and meat strips until chicken is full. Reshape chicken and sew up the back with thread.

Place 1 slice salt pork on the bottom of an oval terrine or a casserole and add the bay leaf and thyme. Pour in the water and brandy. Arrange the stuffed chicken on top and cover with remaining salt pork. Sprinkle with remaining salt and pepper. If there are any open spaces between chicken and terrine, fill them with any remaining stuffing. Cover terrine and seal rim with flour-and-water paste. Cook in a 300° oven 2½ hours. Remove from oven and allow to cool completely before opening terrıne. Serve cold, in slices.

Note: It is just a little difficult to cut even slices because of the bones; if you wish, cut away the part with the bones.

Serves 8-10.

POULARDE À LA CRÈME

Chicken in Cream

2 tablespoons butter
1 4-pound chicken, disjointed
1 teaspoon salt
¼ teaspoon freshly ground black pepper
1 small onion, chopped
¾ cup dry white wine
3 tablespoons dry sherry
Bouquet garni (or 1 bay leaf, sprig parsley, and piece celery, tied together)
1 cup heavy cream
Juice of ½ lemon
8 sautéed mushroom caps
1 truffle, sliced (optional)

Melt the butter in a large shallow saucepan, add the chicken, salt, pepper, and onion. Cook, turning pieces several times, for 5 minutes. Reduce heat to low, cover pan, and allow chicken to steam and cook slowly 20 minutes. Stir in the white wine mixed with 2 tablespoons sherry, add bouquet garni, and cook very gently 15 minutes more, or until tender.

Reduce the cream to half over high heat, stirring continually. Season with salt and pepper and add lemon juice. Arrange chicken on a hot serving dish and garnish with mushrooms and pieces of truffle. Add reduced cream to juices in pan and stir in remaining sherry. Check seasoning, adding a little salt if necessary. Strain sauce over chicken and serve very hot.

Serves 4.

POULET BRETON

Brittany Creamed Chicken

1 3½-pound chicken, disjointed
3 tablespoons butter
Salt, freshly ground black pepper
1 leek, white part only, finely sliced
1 onion, finely sliced
1 tablespoon cider or apple brandy
½ cup heavy cream

Put the chicken in a saucepan with the butter and season with salt and pepper. Cover and cook over medium heat, turning often, until tender. The chicken should not brown. When almost done, add the leek and onion and continue cooking until vegeatbles are soft. Transfer chicken to a hot serving platter. Stir cider or brandy into the pan and add cream. Simmer 2 minutes and pour sauce over chicken.

Serves 4.

FRICASSÉE DE POULET À L'AUVERGNATE

Chicken Fricassee, Auvergne Fashion

1 4-pound roasting chicken, disjointed
1 slice of bacon
1 onion, sliced
1 carrot, sliced
1 small stalk celery with leaves
2 cloves garlic
2 cloves
1 bay leaf
½ teaspoon thyme
Large sprig of parsley
2 tablespoons vinegar
1½ cups water
1 teaspoon salt
¼ teaspoon freshly ground black pepper
4 tablespoon butter
1 tablespoon flour
¼ pound mushrooms, sliced and sautéed
1 teaspoon chopped parsley
1 egg yolk

Put the chicken parts in an earthenware casserole with the bacon, onion, carrot, celery, garlic, cloves, bay leaf, thyme, parsley sprig, vinegar, water, salt, pepper, and 2 tablespoons butter. Cover and bake in a 375° oven 45 minutes or until chicken is done.

Remove chicken and strain stock. There should be about 1½ cups liquid. Melt the remaining butter in a saucepan, blend in flour, and gradually add hot stock, stirring to the boiling point. Cook, stirring steadily, 5 minutes. Return chicken and simmer 5 minutes. Add mushrooms and chopped parsley. Beat egg yolk and mix into it a little hot sauce, stirring steadily to prevent curdling. Return to balance of sauce and reheat but do not boil. Correct seasoning and remove bay leaf.

Serves 4.

FRICASSÉE DE POULET

CHICKEN FRICASSEE, FAMILY STYLE

1 4-pound chicken, disjointed
2 tablespoons butter
2 tablespoons flour
4 cups water
10 small white onions
2 teaspoons salt
¼ teaspoon white pepper
3 sprigs parsley
1 bay leaf
½ pound mushrooms, washed and dried
1 egg yolk
2 tablespoons heavy cream
1 teaspoon lemon juice
Parsley sprigs

Wash and dry the chicken. Melt the butter in a heavy saucepan and stir in the flour. Add the water, stirring to the boiling point. Add the chicken, onions, salt, pepper, parsley, and bay leaf. CCover and cook over medium heat 45 minutes. Add the mushrooms (caps only) and cook 15 minutes longer.

Transfer chicken to a hot serving platter and surround with the onions and mushrooms. Strain sauce. Beat egg yolk with cream and add a little of the hot sauce, stirring steadily to prevent curdling. Add to balance of sauce in pan and heat but do not allow to boil. Mix in the lemon juice and pour sauce over chicken. Remove bay leaf. Garnish with parsley.

Serves 4-6.

FRICASSÉE DE POULET AU CHABLIS

Chicken Fricassee with White Wine

1 4-pound roasting chicken, disjointed
Salt, freshly ground black pepper
4 tablespoons butter
1 tablespoon flour
1 clove garlic, crushed
1 cup Chablis or similar dry white wine
1 cup chicken stock
2 shallots, chopped
Bouquet garni (1 bay leaf, thyme, parsley)
2 egg yolks
3 tablespoons heavy cream
1 tablespoon sweet butter
Juice of 1 small lemon
8 mushrooms, sautéed

Season the chicken with salt and pepper. Melt the butter in a large heavy pan and brown the chicken pieces lightly on all sides. Sprinkle with the flour. Add the garlic. Mix in the wine and stock. Stir to the boiling point. Add shallots and bouquet garni. Cover pan and cook in a 350° oven 30 minutes, or until chicken is tender.

Transfer chicken to a deep hot serving dish and keep warm. Reduce sauce to half over high heat. Beat the egg yolks with the cream. Stir a little of the hot sauce into the egg yolk mixture, stirring steadily to prevent curdling. Return to pan and add butter. Add lemon juice and sautéed mushrooms. Reheat but do not boil. Taste for seasoning. Pour sauce over chicken and serve.

Serves 4-6.

POULET NIVERNAIS

Chicken with Dumplings

2 3-pound fryers, disjointed
4 teaspoons salt
½ teaspoon freshly ground black pepper
4 ounces butter
12 small white onions
2 cloves
1 cup sliced mushrooms
1¼ cups dry white wine
1 bay leaf
1 clove garlic, minced
½ teaspoon marjoram
¼ teaspoon thyme
½ teaspoon saffron
1 cup sour cream, scalded
1½ cups sifted flour
2 teaspoons baking powder
2 eggs
⅓ cup milk
1 tablespoon minced parsley

Season the chicken pieces with 3 teaspoons salt and the pepper. Melt the butter in a casserole and brown the chicken. Stud 1 onion with the cloves. Add all the onions and the mushrooms to the casserole and cook 5 minutes over low heat. Mix in the wine, bay leaf, garlic, marjoram, and thyme. Cover and cook in a 375° oven 45 minutes or until almost tender. Remove from oven, place over low heat. Dissolve the saffron in a little water. Stir in. Carefully stir in the sour cream, a little at a time, blending in well. Correct seasoning.

Sift into a bowl the flour, baking powder, and remaining salt. Beat the eggs. Beat into the flour with the milk. Drop mixture around the edge of the casserole by teaspoons. Cover and cook 15 minutes. Sprinkle top with parsley.

Serves 8-10.

TOURTIÈRE À LA POITEVINE

Chicken Pie

1 3-pound frying chicken
4 tablespoons butter
Salt, freshly ground black pepper
½ cup chicken stock or consommé
¼ pound sausage meat
Chicken liver and heart, chopped
1 teaspoon chopped parsley
1 teaspoon chopped chives
Flaky Pastry (see recipe)
2 hard-cooked eggs, quartered

Remove wings from chicken and reserve for another use. Bone chicken. To do this, first cut off the drumsticks, sever tendons against the bone, loosen meat at the large end with a boning knife, and pull off meat in one piece. Do the same with second joints. Starting at breastbone, lift meat with left hand and free from the carcass with a sawing, scraping motion. This will give you six good pieces of meat, two each from the drumstick, second joint, and breast.

Melt 3 tablespoons butter in a skillet, add the chicken pieces, and sauté until a light brown, turning to cook all sides. Season with salt and pepper. Add the stock, cover, and cook over low heat only 15 minutes.

Combine sausage meat, chopped chicken liver and heart, chopped parsley and chives. Form into 8 balls. Brown in the remaining butter in another pan.

Line an 8-inch pie dish with pie dough. Put in the pieces of chicken and intersperse them with sausage balls and hard-cooked egg quarters. Strain the stock over the chicken mixture. Cover with a top layer of dough. Moisten dough edges with water and pinch them together. Cut a small hole in the center of the dough. Bake in a 350° oven 30 minutes or until pastry is browned.

Serves 4-6.

LE COQ EN PÂTE

Chicken Pie, Franche-Comté Style

1 4-pound roasting chicken
1 teaspoon salt
¼ teaspoon freshly ground pepper
Pinch nutmeg
Pinch ground cloves
Pinch cinnamon
1 carrot, sliced
2 onions
4 tablespoons butter
1 pair sweetbreads, parboiled (see recipe)
½ cup diced cooked ham
¼ pound mushrooms, sliced
Juice of ½ lemon
¼ cup brandy
¾ cup port
2 cups heavy cream
1 tablespoon pâté de foie gras
Flaky Pastry for top crust (see recipe)

Put the chicken in a casserole with its giblets, salt, pepper, nutmeg, cloves, cinnamon, carrot, onions, and 2 tablespoons butter. Bake uncovered in a 375° oven about 1½ hours, or until tender.

Meanwhile, remove skin and tubes from sweetbreads and slice. Cook the ham and mushrooms for a few minutes in the remaining butter and the lemon juice. Combine with the sweetbreads.

Remove chicken from casserole and cut into serving pieces. Arrange in a deep baking dish; add the vegetables and liquid in which chicken was cooked. Stir brandy, port, and cream into casserole and taste for seasoning, adding a little salt if necessary. Strain into a saucepan, add the sweetbread mixture, and simmer 4 minutes. Stir in *pâté de foie gras*. Turn mixture into baking dish, cover top with flaky pie dough, and bake in a 450° oven for 20 minutes, or until crust is golden brown.

Serves 6.

POULET DE BRESSE À LA NANTUA

Chicken with Lobster Sauce

6 cups water
1 onion
1 small carrot
Bouquet garni (1 bay leaf, thyme, parsley)
2½ teaspoons salt
½ teaspoon freshly ground pepper
1 3½-pound chicken
1 lobster (about 1 pound), cooked, or small can lobster meat
¼ pound mushrooms, sliced
Lemon juice
3 tablespoons butter
2 tablespoons flour
¾ cup cream
1 truffle, sliced (optional)

Put the water, onion, carrot, bouquet garni, salt and pepper in a saucepan and bring to a boil. Reduce heat and simmer 30 minutes. Put the chicken in this court-bouillon and poach over very low heat for 2 hours, or until done. Remove chicken (reserve the stock), cut into serving pieces, remove skin, and arrange on a hot serving dish. Keep warm while preparing the sauce.

For *Sauce Nantua* (lobster sauce), shell the lobster and cut the meat into slices. Reserve. Simmer the mushrooms in a little salted water with a few drops lemon juice for 10 minutes. Strain. Mix liquid into chicken stock and reduce liquids to 2 cups over high heat.

Melt butter in a saucepan and blend in flour. Gradually add reduced stock, stirring to the boiling point. Cook sauce a few minutes, then add the cream. Simmer 1 minute; add sliced lobster meat and truffle. Pour sauce over chicken and serve. Serves 6.

VOLAILLE BEYNAC

Chicken, Beynac Style

½ pound veal
1 veal bone
2 shallots
1 clove garlic
1 quart water
2 cups dry white wine
Salt, freshly ground black pepper
1 3½-pound chicken, disjointed
2 tablespoons goose fat or bacon drippings
1 truffle, sliced
¼ cup brandy
2 tablespoons Madeira
4 mushrooms, sliced

Put in a large kettle the veal, veal bone, shallots, garlic, water, wine, and salt and pepper to taste. Cover and simmer 2 hours. Strain the stock.

Brown the chicken all over in the goose fat or bacon drippings. Add to strained stock, with juices from pan in which chicken was cooked, sliced truffle and juice from its can, brandy, Madeira, and mushrooms. Simmer 45 minutes. Serve hot.

Serves 4.

POULET À LA MODE DE ROQUEFORT

Chicken with Roquefort Cheese

2 1½-pound broilers, split
1½ teaspoons salt
¼ teaspoon freshly ground black pepper
3 tablespoons butter
6 ounces Roquefort cheese
1 clove garlic, minced
1½ cups sour cream

Rub the broilers with the salt and pepper. Melt the butter in a skillet. Brown the chickens and remove and arrange in a baking dish.

Mash the cheese with a fork. Blend with the garlic and sour cream. Spread over the chicken. Cover. Bake in a 375°

oven until chicken is tender, about 30 minutes, removing cover for last 5 minutes.

Serves 4.

CRÊPES NIÇOISES

Chicken-stuffed Pancakes

1 recipe crêpes (see recipe)
¾ cup sliced mushrooms
6 tablespoons butter
¾ cup diced cooked chicken or turkey
3 hard-cooked egg yolks, mashed
4 tablespoons sour cream
1 tablespoon minced parsley
¾ teaspoon salt
¼ teaspoon freshly ground white pepper
3 tablespoons grated Parmesan cheese

Make the crêpes, stack and keep warm while preparing filling.

Sauté the mushrooms in 3 tablespoons butter for 5 minutes. Remove from heat. Combine with the chicken, egg yolks, sour cream, parsley, and salt and pepper. Taste for seasoning. Spread the filling evenly on the crêpes and roll up. Arrange in a buttered baking dish and sprinkle with the cheese. Dot with the rest of the butter and bake in a preheated 475° oven until delicately browned, about 5 minutes.

Makes about 16.

CANETON NANTAIS

Roast Duck, Nantes Style

1 6-pound duck
Salt, freshly ground black pepper
2 pounds peas, shelled
12 small white onions
1 tablespoon butter
2 tablespoons diced lean bacon
¼ teaspoon savory or thyme
½ cup strong chicken stock

Season the duck with salt and pepper. Roast in a 375° oven 2 hours, draining the fat frequently.

While it is roasting, cook the peas in boiling salted water and drain. Sauté the onions in the butter until golden; add the diced bacon and sauté together 3 minutes.

After duck has cooked for 1½ hours, pour off the fat from the roasting pan and add the cooked peas, onions and bacon, and savory. Season to taste with salt and pepper, add the stock, and continue cooking until duck is done.

Serves 4.

CANARD AUX OLIVES PROVENÇAL

Duck with Olives

Veal bones
1 teaspoon salt
½ teaspoon freshly ground black pepper
1 bay leaf
2 sprigs parsley
Pinch of thyme
1 onion
1 cup dry white wine
2 tablespoons tomato paste
1 tablespoon butter blended with 1 tablespoon flour
1 5-pound duckling, disjointed
2 tablespoons butter
2 tablespoons warmed brandy
12 small pitted green Italian olives
Triangles of French bread, sautéed in butter

Make a veal stock by simmering the veal bones in water to cover with salt, pepper, bay leaf, parsley, thyme, and onion for 2 hours, adding the wine after 1½ hours of cooking. (If you do not have veal bones, use any good light stock and add the herbs and wine.) Reduce stock to about 1½ cups and strain. Thicken strained stock by stirring in the tomato paste and butter mixed with flour. Brown the duck parts over low heat in a pan with the butter. Pour off the fat; set brandy aflame and pour over the duck. Cover and cook 30 minutes. Add the veal stock and olives; simmer 10 minutes. Serve very hot with sautéed French bread.

Serves 4.

CANARD AU VIN ROUGE

Duck in Red Wine

1 5-pound duck
2 teaspoons salt
½ teaspoon pepper
3 tablespoons butter
3 tablespoons flour
1 cup chicken stock
1 cup dry red wine
1 tablespoon chopped onion
1 teaspoon chopped parsley
2 teaspoons grated orange rind
¼ teaspoon rosemary
1 bay leaf
Duck liver

Wash the duck, dry, and season with the salt and pepper. Chop the liver and reserve. Place duck on a rack in a shallow pan; roast in a 375° oven 1½ hours. Carve the duck into serving-sized pieces, removing as many bones as possible.

Melt the butter in a saucepan and mix in the flour until browned. Add stock and wine, stirring to the boiling point. Add the carved duck, the onion, parsley, orange rind, rosemary, and bay leaf. Cook over low heat 1 hour. Discard bay leaf. Stir the liver into the sauce; cook 5 minutes. Serve on rounds of toasted bread.

Serves 4-5.

PIGEONS EN COMPOTE

Squab Casserole

2 1¼-pound squabs
2 tablespoons butter
¼ pound salt pork or bacon, diced
2 tablespoons flour
2 cups chicken stock
½ teaspoon salt
¼ teaspoon freshly ground black pepper
½ teaspoon thyme
1 bay leaf
10 small white onions
¼ pound mushrooms
10 pitted green olives
Large croutons
Parsley sprigs

Split the squabs in half lengthwise. Heat the butter in a heavy pan. When sizzling, add squabs and brown on both sides, then remove. Add salt pork and let brown. Stir in the flour until browned, add the stock, stirring to the boiling point. Add salt, pepper, thyme, bay leaf, and onions. Replace squabs and cook over medium heat 30 minutes. Add mushrooms (caps only) and olives. Cook 15 minutes longer. Transfer squabs to a deep hot serving platter. Discard bay leaf and pour sauce over squabs. Garnish with croutons and parsley.

Serves 4.

CASSEROLE DE PIGEONS LIÉGEOISE

Squab with Vegetables

4 pigeons or squabs
2 teaspoons salt
½ teaspoon freshly ground black pepper
4 tablespoons butter
3 carrots, quartered lengthwise
1 cup cubed potatoes
12 green onions (scallions)
4 slices bacon, half cooked and crumbled
1 cup shelled fresh or frozen thawed peas
¼ teaspoon thyme
½ cup boiling water

Wash and dry the birds and season with the salt and pepper. Melt the butter in a casserole and brown the birds well all over. Add the carrots, potatoes, green onions, and bacon and sauté 5 minutes. Stir in the peas, thyme, and water, cover casserole tightly, and cook 1 hour in a 325° oven, or until tender. Skim fat off top, adjust seasoning and serve.

Serves 4.

DINDE À LA STRASBOURGEOISE

Roast Stuffed Turkey, Strasbourg Style

1 10-pound turkey
4 teaspoons salt
¾ teaspoon freshly ground black pepper
1 clove garlic, minced
½ pound chicken livers, chopped
1½ pounds ground pork
1 egg, beaten
3 black truffles, sliced
4 tablespoons butter
1½ cups dry white wine
½ pound mushrooms, sliced

Clean, wash, and dry the turkey. Combine 2 teaspoons salt, ½ teaspoon pepper, and the garlic, and rub the turkey with the mixture. Mix well together the livers, pork, egg, truffles, and remaining salt and pepper, and stuff the turkey. Skewer openings and truss turkey. Melt the butter in a shallow roasting pan and put the turkey in. Roast in a 350° oven 1½ hours. Add the wine and mushrooms and roast 1 hour, basting often.

Serves 8-10.

DINDONNEAU À LA BRETONNE

Turkey with Sausage-Prune Stuffing

1 10-pound turkey
1 tablespoon salt
½ teaspoon freshly ground black pepper
1 pound sausage meat
1 cup seedless raisins, soaked 6 hours in 1 cup port
20 pitted prunes, cooked
Pinch of thyme

Season the turkey inside and out with the salt and pepper. Break the sausage meat into pieces and cook in a frying pan until browned. Heat the raisins in the port until slightly plumped. Pour off excess fat from sausage meat and add the raisins, drained prunes, thyme, and the turkey liver, chopped.

Mix well together. Stuff turkey with the mixture and roast in a 375° oven 2½ hours or until tender.

Serves 10-12.

OIE À L'ALSACIENNE

Goose with Sauerkraut

1 10-12 pound goose
Salt, freshly ground black pepper
2 onions, sliced
2 tablespoons butter
2 pounds sausage meat
2 cups fresh bread crumbs
2 pounds sauerkraut
4 thick slices lean bacon
6 large frankfurters
¾ cup dry white wine
¾ cup beef stock

Wash and dry the goose. Season inside and out with salt and pepper.

Sauté the onions in the butter until golden, then mix well with the sausage meat and bread crumbs. Stuff goose with this mixture, truss and roast in a 325° oven, allowing 25 minutes per pound, or until tender. Pour off the fat as it accumulates.

Meanwhile, drain sauerkraut, put in a deep pan, and cover with boiling water. (Drain again and add fresh boiling water if you prefer not to have the sauerkraut too strong.) Add the bacon and ¼ cup of the fat from the roasting goose, cover the pan, and braise the sauerkraut 1 hour or more. During the last half hour, lay the frankfurters on the sauerkraut.

Transfer the goose to a hot serving platter and surround with the sauerkraut topped with the bacon and sliced frankfurters.

Skim fat from roasting pan and add wine and stock. Reduce a little and serve the sauce separately with the goose and sauerkraut.

Serves 6-8.

Meat

Meat

BOEUF RÔTI À LA BORDELAISE

Roast Beef, Bordeaux Fashion

3-pound rump roast of beef
1 onion, sliced
2 shallots, chopped
4 sprigs parsley
1 bay leaf
½ teaspoon thyme
½ cup olive oil
1 cup dry white wine
1 teaspoon salt
½ teaspoon freshly ground black pepper
1 tablespoon wine vinegar

Remove fat from meat and reserve. Marinate meat overnight in a mixture of the onion, shallots, parsley, bay leaf, thyme, oil, wine, salt and pepper.

Put a strip of the reserved beef fat in the bottom of a roasting pan. Strain marinade (reserving it) and put vegetables and herbs on fat. Put meat on top, season all over with some salt and pepper, place another piece of fat over it, and add 3 tablespoons strained marinade. Roast at 350° 1¼ hours, basting often. Transfer meat to a serving platter and keep hot.

Strain juices from roasting pan and combine in a saucepan with remaining strained marinade. Cook until reduced a little, allow to stand a few minutes, and skim fat from top. Add wine vinegar, reheat, and serve separately as a sauce for roast.

Serves 6-8.

BOEUF BOUILLI À LA BORDELAISE

Beef, Bordeaux Style

1 tablespoon butter
1 onion, chopped
12 thin slices of cold boiled or roast beef
¼ teaspoon salt
¼ teaspoon freshly ground black pepper
1 shallot, chopped
1 clove garlic, chopped and mashed
¼ cup beef stock
⅓ cup dry white wine
1 tablespoon chopped parsley

Melt the butter in a skillet, add the onion, beef slices, salt and pepper. Sauté the beef on both sides until brown. Add the shallot, garlic, stock, wine, and parsley, and simmer until the sauce is reduced—there should be just enough left to coat the beef.

Serves 4.

FILET DE BOEUF EN CROUSTADE

Beef Fillet in Crust

4-pound fillet of beef
Strips of salt pork
2 tablespoons butter
1 onion, sliced
2 carrots, sliced
2 sprigs parsley
1 bay leaf
⅛ teaspoon sage
¼ teaspoon thyme
⅛ teaspoon nutmeg
1½ cups dry white wine
½ pound mushrooms, chopped and sautéed
¼ pound ham, chopped and sautéed
2 slices bacon, browned and chopped
¼ pound chicken livers, chopped and sautéed
Salt, freshly ground black pepper
1 egg, beaten
1 tablespoon brandy
Flaky Pastry (see recipe)
1 to 2 tablespoons Madeira

Lard the tenderloin with salt pork strips. Melt the butter, add the onion, carrots, parsley, bay leaf, sage, thyme, and nutmeg. Cover and cook 5 minutes. Combine with the wine, add the fillet and marinate 24 hours, basting with the marinade from time to time.

Mix together chopped sautéed mushrooms, ham, bacon, and chicken livers and season with a little salt and pepper. Mix in the beaten egg and 2 tablespoons of the marinade. Add brandy. Remove the tenderloin from the marinade, wipe dry, and cover completely with a ½-inch layer of the chicken liver mixture. Wrap in flaky pie dough. Moisten edges of dough with water and seal well. Cut 2 or 3 small holes in the top. Place on a baking pan.

Bake in a 425° oven for about 15 minutes per pound for rare beef, 20 minutes per pound for medium, pouring the Madeira through the holes in the crust toward the end of the cooking time. Turn off oven and allow to stand 15 minutes before serving. Serve with sautéed potatoes.

Serves 6-8.

TOURNEDOS DAUPHINOIS

Fillets of Beef with Port Wine Sauce

¾ pound firm white mushrooms, sliced
¼ pound butter
Salt, freshly ground black pepper
2 teaspoons flour
1 cup heavy cream, warmed
6 fillets of beef, cut ¾ inch thick
6 slices of French bread, ½ inch thick
½ cup port or sherry

Sauté the mushrooms in 3 tablespoons butter. Sprinkle with salt, pepper, and flour, blend, and stir in cream. Keep hot.

Quickly sauté fillets in 3 tablespoons hot butter for 2 minutes on each side. Sauté French bread in 2 tablespoons butter, turning often to prevent one side absorbing all the butter. Place fillets on sautéed bread and arrange in a ring on a hot platter. Put mushroom mixture in center. Stir port into juices in pan used to cook meat, boil up once or twice, and pour a spoonful on each fillet. Serve rest of sauce separately.

Serves 6.

FILET DE BOEUF BRAISÉ

Braised Fillet of Beef

4-pound fillet of beef
1½ teaspoons salt
¼ teaspoon freshly ground black pepper
2 tablespoons olive oil
1 cup thinly sliced carrots
1½ cups thinly sliced onions
1 bay leaf

Have the butcher wrap the fillet in a thin sheet of beef fat. Rub with the salt and pepper.

Heat the oil in a heavy casserole or Dutch oven and spread a layer of the carrots and onions over the bottom. Add the bay leaf. Arrange fillet on top, cover, and cook over medium heat 30 minutes or to desired degree of rareness, turning frequently so the meat cooks evenly. At the end of 30 minutes the meat will be cooked rare, so if you prefer it cooked more, adjust time accordingly. Serve with sautéed mushroom caps.

Serves 6-8.

FILET MIGNON LYONNAIS

Fillet of Beef on Toast

4 fillets of beef, 1 inch thick
4 tablespoons butter
1 teaspoon salt
¼ teaspoon freshly ground black pepper
4 slices of French bread, sautéed in butter
2 tablespoons chopped shallots
1 teaspoon anchovy paste
½ cup dry white wine

Brown the fillets in 3 tablespoons hot butter over high heat, 4 minutes on each side. Season with the salt and pepper.

Arrange on the sautéed bread on a serving platter and keep warm. To the pan juices add the shallots, anchovy paste, wine, and remaining butter. Mix well and cook 2 minutes over medium heat. Spoon over the fillets.

Serves 4.

ÉMINCÉ DE BOEUF BOURGEOIS

Sliced Beef with Chicken Liver Sauce

2-pound fillet of beef
4 tablespoons butter
½ pound chicken livers
1 bay leaf
1 teaspoon salt
¼ teaspoon thyme
¼ teaspoon freshly ground black pepper
½ cup beef stock
2 tablespoons brandy

Cut the fillet in thin strips across the grain. Set aside.

Heat 2 tablespoons butter in a skillet, add the livers and bay leaf, and sauté 3 minutes over high heat. Sprinkle with the salt, thyme, and pepper and sauté 2 minutes more. Discard bay leaf. Put livers in electric blender with beef stock and purée until smooth. Keep warm in skillet.

Melt the remaining butter in a skillet, add the beef, and sauté over high heat 2 minutes, shaking the pan so the meat browns on all sides. Warm brandy and flame the beef with it. Put beef on a hot serving dish, pour liver sauce over, and serve.

Serves 6-8.

BOEUF SAUTÉ LYONNAIS

Sautéed Beef Lyonnaise

1½ pounds fillet of beef or sirloin steak
1½ cups thinly sliced onions
5 tablespoons butter
1½ teaspoons salt
¼ teaspoon freshly ground black pepper
1 tablespoon minced parsley
1 teaspoon wine vinegar

Cut the fillet into slices ¼ inch thick or have the piece of sirloin cut ¼-inch thick and slice it into 4 or 6 pieces.

Sauté the onions in a skillet in 2 tablespoons hot butter until lightly browned. Remove, add remaining butter, and brown the beef all over. Return onions to skillet, season with salt and pepper, and cook 5 minutes over low heat. Sprinkle with parsley and vinegar.

Serves 4.

TOURNEDOS LYONNAIS

Beef Tenderloin Lyonnaise

4 fillets of beef, cut 1 inch thick
Salt, freshly ground black pepper
4 tablespoons butter
4 slices of French bread, sautéed in butter until browned
1 shallot, chopped
½ cup dry white wine
1 teaspoon anchovy paste

Season the fillets with salt and pepper and brown in 3 tablespoons butter, allowing 2 to 3 minutes on each side. Do no overcook. Place each fillet on a slice of sautéed bread. Add shallot to butter in pan after removing meat, and stir in the wine and anchovy paste blended with the remaining tablespoon butter. Mix together thoroughly and simmer 2 minutes. Pour sauce over fillets and serve with sautéed potatoes.

Serves 4.

Tournedos Bordelais

Prepare Tournedos as directed above, but serve with Sauce Bordelaise (see recipe).

ENTRECÔTE GRILLÉ BOURGUIGNON

GRILLED STEAK, BURGUNDY STYLE

1 tablespoon butter
1 tablespoon finely chopped onions
½ teaspoon flour
1 cup dry red wine
2 cloves garlic, minced
1 tablespoon tomato paste
1 tablespoon Madeira or sweet sherry
1 Delmonico or club steak, 2 inches thick

Melt the butter in a skillet and sauté the onions until soft but not brown. Blend in the flour. Slowly add the wine and stir to the boiling point. Add the garlic, tomato paste, and Madeira. Simmer over low heat 30 minutes.

Preheat broiler. Broil steak quickly, until brown on outside but still rare and juicy inside. Serve with the red wine sauce.

Serves 2-3.

LE HACHUA

BRAISED BEEF, PYRENEES STYLE

4 tablespoons lard or goose or bacon fat
3 pounds stewing beef, cut in ¾-inch cubes
2 cups chopped onions
2 cloves garlic, minced
1½ cups finely diced ham
2 tablespoons flour
3 sprigs parsley
1 bay leaf
½ teaspoon thyme
2 teaspoons salt
½ teaspoon freshly ground pepper
1¾ cups hot water
1 cup dry white wine
3 green peppers, cut in ½-inch pieces

Melt the fat in a heavy pan or Dutch oven and brown the beef all over. Add onions, garlic, ham, flour, parsley, bay leaf, thyme, salt and pepper. Gradually stir in water and wine. Cover tightly and cook in a 275° oven 2½ hours or until meat is tender, adding green peppers half an hour before serving.

Serves 6-8.

BOEUF À LA MODE—I

Braised Beef and Vegetables

4 pounds eye round of beef
2 tablespoons butter or oil
3 cups water
½ cup dry white wine
¼ cup brandy
2 cloves
12 small white onions
2 carrots, diced
4 sprigs parsley
1 bay leaf
½ teaspoon thyme
2 teaspoons salt
¼ teaspoon freshly ground black pepper
½ calf's foot or 1 veal knuckle

Have the butcher lard the beef with strips of salt pork, or wrap 2 pieces of bacon around it.

Melt the butter in a deep, heavy casserole and sear the meat on all sides. Add the water, wine, and brandy. Stick the cloves in 1 onion. Add all the onions, the carrots, parsley, bay leaf, thyme, salt, pepper, and calf's foot. Bring to a boil. Cover casserole and bake in a 300° oven 4 hours. To serve, place meat on a hot serving platter. Discard parsley, bay leaf, and calf's foot. Skim fat from sauce and spoon vegetables and sauce around the meat.

Serves 8-10.

ESTOUFFAT CATALANE

BRAISED STEW, CATALAN MANNER

5 pound eye round of beef
Strips of salt pork or bacon
1 clove garlic, slivered
Vinegar
Flour
2 slices bacon, diced
2 onions, sliced
2 carrots, cut in strips
2 small white turnips, peeled and quartered
3 tomatoes, skinned, seeded, and coarsely chopped
3 sprigs parsley
1 bay leaf
½ teaspoon thyme
1 clove garlic, minced
2 cloves
1 teaspoon salt
½ teaspoon freshly ground black pepper
1 quart dry red wine
2 cups cooked white beans

Wrap the beef with the salt pork and insert the garlic slivers. Brush all over with vinegar, roll in flour, and put in a deep heavy pan with the bacon, onions, carrots, turnips, tomatoes, parsley, bay leaf, thyme, garlic, cloves, salt and pepper. Add the wine, cover pan tightly, and bake in a 275° oven 4 hours. When beef is almost cooked, add kidney beans, and simmer 10 minutes longer. Discard bay leaf.

Serves 8-10.

BOEUF EN MIROTON

PEASANT BEEF STEW

2 tablespoons butter
2 tablespoons flour
2 cups beef stock or water
1 teaspoon salt
½ teaspoon black pepper
12 small white onions
6 potatoes, peeled and quartered
2 sprigs parsley
¼ teaspoon thyme
1 bay leaf
4 cups cooked boiled beef, cut in small pieces

Melt the butter in a saucepan and add the flour; cook, stirring steadily until browned. Slowly mix in the stock or water, stirring to the boiling point. Season with the salt and pepper, add the onions, potatoes, parsley, thyme, and bay leaf. Simmer 45 minutes. Add beef. Simmer 15 minutes longer. Remove parsley and bay leaf and serve.

Serves 6.

LA CARBONNADE

Beef Stew, Languedoc Style

1 cup rice
3 ears corn or 1 cup canned or frozen corn
2½ pounds rump steak, cut into large dice
2 tablespoons butter
1 Large onion, sliced
2 ripe tomatoes, skinned and sliced
1 teaspoon salt
¼ teaspoon freshly ground pepper
½ cup finely sliced green pepper
¼ teaspoon saffron
¾ teaspoon brown sugar
1 cup dry white wine
Pinch cinnamon

Cook rice in boiling salted water until tender. Drain. Cook corn in boiling salted water 3 minutes, drain and cut off kernels. (If canned or frozen corn is used, do not cook.) Combine rice and corn kernels and reserve.

Brown beef cubes in hot butter. Add onion and tomatoes, season with salt and pepper, cover and cook over high heat 10 minutes, shaking pan occasionally so meat will not stick. Mix in rice and corn, green pepper, saffron, sugar, wine, and cinnamon. Cover and cook over medium heat 20 minutes.

Serves 6.

L'ESTOUFFAT DE BOEUF

BEEF STEW, GASCONY STYLE

3- to 4-pound piece lean beef (eye of round)
2 cloves garlic, slivered
Salt, freshly ground pepper
1 slice fresh pork rind or bacon
Pinch cinnamon
Pinch nutmeg
3 cloves
Bouquet garni (or bay leaf, sprig parsley, and piece celery, tied together)
1 onion, quartered
2 carrots, cut in long strips
1 tablespoon diced bacon
2 shallots
¼ cup brandy
½ cup beef stock
2 cups dry red wine

Stick the garlic slivers into the beef and rub it all over with salt and pepper. Put the pork rind or bacon in a large casserole and place the beef on top. Add the cinnamon, nutmeg, cloves, bouquet garni, onion, carrots, diced bacon, shallots, brandy, stock, and wine. The beef should be practically covered. Cover casserole with a piece of heavy waxed paper and tie securely. Cover with lid and cook in a 350° oven 1 hour. Reduce heat to 250° and cook at least 6 hours longer.

Note: This dish is improved if cooked in advance and reheated 1 hour. Skim fat from top before serving.

Serves 6-8.

BOEUF À LA BOURGUIGNONNE

BEEF, BURGUNDY STYLE

3 pounds cross rib or chuck
½ cup flour
2 teaspoons salt
¼ teaspoon freshly ground black pepper
3 tablespoons olive oil
6 tablespoons butter
¼ cup warm cognac
3 slices bacon, diced
2 cups diced onions
¾ cup grated carrots
2 cloves garlic, minced or ½ teaspoon garlic powder
3 cups dry red wine
2 tablespoons minced parsley
1 bay leaf
½ teaspoon thyme
12 small white onions
1 teaspoon sugar
12 mushroom caps

Cut the meat into 2-inch cubes; roll in a mixture of the flour, salt, and pepper. Heat the oil and 3 tablespoons butter in a skillet; brown the meat very well on all sides. Transfer to a casserole or Dutch oven; pour warm cognac over it and set aflame.

To the skillet add the bacon, diced onions, carrots, and garlic. Cook over medium heat until vegetables brown. Add to the meat with the wine, parsley, bay leaf, and thyme. Cover and bake in a 350° oven 2 hours. While the meat is cooking prepare the onions and mushrooms.

Melt the remaining butter in a skillet; add the onions and sugar. Brown lightly. Remove and sauté the mushrooms 5 minutes. Add to the meat after 1½ hours of baking. Taste for seasoning.

Note: The meat may be cooked over direct low heat if you prefer.

Serves 6-8.

RAGOÛT DE BOEUF BORDELAIS

MARINATED BEEF STEW

3 pounds cross rib, chuck, or rump
1 clove garlic, minced
2 teaspoons salt
½ teaspoon freshly ground black pepper
2 cloves
1 bay leaf
¼ teaspoon thyme
1 cup dry red wine
¼ cup olive oil
2 cups beef stock
3 sprigs parsley
12 small white onions
3 carrots, cut in 2-inch pieces
12 firm mushroom caps
1 cup cooked green beans

Cut the meat in 2-inch cubes. In a glass or pottery (not metal) bowl, combine the garlic, salt, pepper, cloves, bay leaf, thyme, and wine. Add the meat and marinate 2 hours or overnight. Drain meat. Reserve marinade.

Heat oil in a deep casserole or Dutch oven, add meat, and cook over low heat until very dark brown. Stir in the marinade, stock, and parsley, bring to a boil, and cook over high heat 15 minutes. Cover, reduce heat, and cook 30 minutes over low heat. Add onions, carrots, and mushrooms. Cover and cook over low heat 1½ hours or until tender. Mix in beans, heat, adjust seasoning.

Serves 6-8.

BOEUF À LA MODE—II

FRENCH POT ROAST

3 pounds eye round or rump of beef
1 onion, sliced
1 bay leaf
2 teaspoons salt
½ teaspoon freshly ground black pepper
¼ teaspoon thyme
⅛ teaspoon nutmeg
2 tablespoons wine vinegar
4 tablespoons olive oil
3½ cups dry red wine
1 veal knuckle
2 cloves garlic, minced
3 tablespoons brandy
12 small white onions
Quartered carrots, mushroom caps (optional)

Ask the butcher to lard the beef. Combine in a glass or pottery (not metal) bowl the onion, bay leaf, salt, pepper, thyme, nutmeg, vinegar, 2 tablespoons oil, and 1½ cups wine. Put in the meat and marinate at least 24 hours, turning occasionally. Drain well and reserve marinade.

Heat the remaining oil in a skillet and brown the meat on all sides over high heat. Remove meat and put in a Dutch oven or deep heavy saucepan. Pour the marinade into the skillet and bring to a boil, scraping brown glaze from the bottom of the skillet. Add to the Dutch oven with the veal knuckle, garlic, brandy, and remaining wine. Cover, bring to a boil, and cook in a 350° oven 3 hours. Remove and discard knuckle and skim fat from surface. Add the onions, cover, and cook 1 hour longer. If carrots and mushrooms are used, add them with the onions. Taste for seasoning. Slice meat and arrange on a serving platter, surround with vegetables, and pour some of the gravy over the meat, serving the rest in a sauceboat.

Serves 6-8.

Boeuf à la Mode en Gelée

JELLIED BEEF

Slice the cooked beef thinly and arrange slices in a mold or casserole, overlapping. Strain gravy. Soften 1 envelope (1 tablespoon) gelatin in 2 tablespoons water and stir into the hot gravy until dissolved. Pour over the meat. Chill until firm. Carefully turn out of mold onto a platter.

BOULETTES DE BOEUF

BEEF BALLS

1 pound lean ground beef
¼ pound sausage meat
2 onions, finely chopped
1 teaspoon chopped parsley
2 slices bread soaked in ¼ cup milk
2 eggs
1 teaspoon salt
¼ teaspoon freshly ground black pepper
½ cup flour
¾ cup dry bread crumbs
Fat for deep frying
½ bunch parsley sprigs

Combine in a bowl the beef, sausage meat, onions, and parsley. Add the bread, 1 egg, salt and pepper, and mix thoroughly. Chill. With wet hands, shape the mixture into small balls or ovals. Roll them in the flour, the remaining beaten egg, and finally in the bread crumbs. Heat the fat to 375° and fry the meat balls, turning frequently to brown all over. Remove, drain, and arrange on a hot serving dish. Drop the parsley into the hot fat and remove almost immediately with a skimmer. Garnish the meat balls with the fried parsley.

Serves 4.

BIFTECKS À LA MIREMONDE

Ground Beef, Miremonde Fashion

2 slices stale bread, trimmed
6 tablespoons milk
1 pound ground beef
1 onion, finely chopped and sautéed
2 eggs, beaten
1 tablespoon uncooked cream of wheat or white cornmeal
1 teaspoon salt
¼ teaspoon freshly ground black pepper
⅛ teaspoon grated nutmeg
3 tablespoons butter
¼ cup dry white wine
1 teaspoon chopped parsley

Crumble the bread and moisten with the milk. Combine with the ground beef, sautéed onion, eggs, cream of wheat, and season with salt, pepper, and nutmeg. Mix well. Let stand 1 hour. Form into 4 patties, Cook over low heat in the butter in a covered skillet for about 10 minutes on each side. Transfer to a heated platter and add the wine and parsley to the pan juices. Stir to boiling point and boil 2 minutes. Pour over the beef patties.

Serves 4.

CÔTELETTES DE VEAU LORRAINE

Veal Chops with White Wine Sauce

1 tablespoon butter
½ cup diced lean bacon
4 thin veal chops
¾ teaspoon salt
¼ teaspoon freshly ground black pepper
2 shallots, finely chopped
1 teaspoon chopped parsley
½ cup dry white wine
½ cup veal or chicken stock
2 egg yolks
1 teaspoon lemon juice

Melt the butter in a skillet and sauté the bacon. Add the chops, sprinkle with salt and pepper, and cook 20 minutes, turning from time to time to brown both sides. Remove chops and bacon and keep hot.

Pour off most of fat from pan and add shallots and parsley. Cook, stirring steadily for 1 minute, but do not brown. Mix in wine and stock, stirring to lift glaze from pan. Season with a little salt and pepper. Beat the egg yolks; gradually add the hot sauce, stirring constantly to prevent curdling, then return to pan, stirring steadily. Reheat, stirring, but do not boil. Return chops and bacon to sauce and heat through. Add lemon juice, stir, and serve.

Serves 4.

CÔTELETTES À LA SAINT-GERMAIN-EN-LAYE

Veal Chops with Mustard Sauce

3 tablespoons butter
4 veal chops
2 tablespoons vinegar
1 teaspoon Dijon-style mustard
2 teaspoons soft butter
3 tablespoons cream
2 tablespoons olive oil
½ teaspoon salt
¼ teaspoon freshly ground black pepper
¼ cup finely chopped parsley

Melt the 3 tablespoons butter in a skillet and cook the chops over medium heat 10 minutes on each side, or until tender.

Blend together in a saucepan the vinegar, mustard, the 2 teaspoons soft butter, cream, oil, salt and pepper. Heat, stirring occasionally, but do not boil. Remove cooked veal from pan and arrange on a hot platter. Add mustard mixture to pan in which veal was cooked and heat, stirring in the pan juices and glaze. Pour sauce over veal and sprinkle with parsley.

Serves 4.

CÔTES DE VEAU À LA BONNE FEMME

Veal Chops Bonne Femme

6 veal chops, loin or rib, ¾ inch thick
½ cup flour
1½ teaspoons salt
¼ teaspoon freshly ground white pepper
6 slices bacon
4 tablespoons butter
12 small white onions
¾ cup chicken stock
¼ cup dry white wine

Dip the chops in the flour which has been seasoned with the salt and pepper. Fry the bacon crisp. Pour off bacon fat and drain the bacon on paper towels. Crumble bacon and set aside.

Melt the butter in the skillet in which the bacon was cooked and lightly brown the onions all over. Remove. Add chops to skillet and brown on both sides. Add onions, crumbled bacon, stock, and wine. Cover and cook over low heat 45 minutes or until chops are tender.

Serves 6.

CÔTES DE VEAU QUERCINOIS

Veal Chops, Quercy Style

4 veal chops
2 tablespoons butter
2 tablespoons olive oil
Salt, freshly ground black pepper
2 cloves garlic, chopped
¾ cup boiling water
½ pound mushrooms, sliced

Brown the chops slowly on both sides in the hot butter and oil until tender. Season with salt and pepper. Transfer it to a hot dish and add to the pan juices the garlic, water, and salt and pepper to taste.

Add the mushrooms and simmer gently 5 minutes. Pour over chops and serve.

Serves 4.

CÔTES DE VEAU À LA NÎMOISE

Veal Chops with Eggplant

6 tablespoons olive oil
6 veal chops, loin or rib, ½ inch thick
½ cup dry white wine
1 eggplant, peeled and sliced
¼ cup flour
3 tomatoes, skinned and cut in eighths
1 clove garlic, minced
1½ teaspoons salt
½ teaspoon freshly ground black pepper

Heat 3 tablespoons oil in a skillet, add chops, and sauté over low heat for 35 minutes, or until tender. Remove chops to a hot serving platter. Add wine to pan juices and bring to a boil, scraping the glaze from the bottom of the pan. Pour over the chops.

While chops are cooking, dip eggplant slices in the flour. Heat remaining oil in a skillet and brown the eggplant on both sides. Remove. Add the tomatoes, garlic, salt and pepper to the pan and cook 10 minutes over low heat, stirring frequently. Add eggplant and cook 2 minutes. Cover chops with the eggplant-tomato mixture.

Serves 6.

ESCALOPE POITEVINE

Veal Scallop Poitou

4 tablespoons butter
8 small thin slices of veal
Salt, freshly ground black pepper
8 large mushrooms, sliced
¼ cup port
1 tablespoon butter blended with 1 tablespoon flour
1½ cups heavy cream
Cayenne pepper

Heat the butter in a heavy skillet. Season the veal with salt and pepper and sauté until golden brown on both sides. Remove to a hot serving dish. Add the mushrooms to the butter remaining in the pan and sauté 4 minutes. Stir in the port, reduce a little, and blend in the butter-flour mixture. Add cream and a pinch of cayenne and heat to boiling point. Pour sauce and mushrooms over veal and serve.

Serves 4.

VEAU ROULÉ

Veal Birds

8 veal cutlets, evenly cut, sliced ½ inch thick
¼ pound sausage meat
½ cup minced cooked beef
1 teaspoon salt
¼ teaspoon freshly ground black pepper
2 tablespoons butter
2 tablespoons flour
1½ cups water
½ cup dry white wine
2 teaspoons chopped onions
2 teaspoons chopped parsley

Have the butcher pound the cutlets thin or pound them yourself between two sheets of waxed paper. Chop the sausage meat and minced beef together. Season with the salt and pepper. Spread a thin layer of the mixture on each cutlet and roll up. Tie ends securely with thread. Melt butter in a large skillet and brown veal birds on all sides. Brown only a few at a time; they should not touch or overlap. Remove and keep warm. Stir flour into butter remaining in skillet. Slowly add water and wine, stirring to the boiling point. Add onions and parsley and season to taste with salt and pepper. Reduce heat and simmer 2 minutes. Replace veal birds, cover, and simmer 45 minutes.

Serves 4.

VEAU EN CASSEROLE À LA BORDELAISE

Braised Veal

5-pound loin or fillet of veal
3 tablespoons butter
1½ cups sliced onions
¾ cup thinly sliced carrots
2 teaspoons salt
½ teaspoon rosemary
½ teaspoon freshly ground black pepper
½ cup boiling water

In a Dutch oven or heavy casserole brown the meat in the butter over low heat. Add the onions and carrots and cook until browned. Season with salt, rosemary, and pepper and add the water. Cover and cook over low heat 2½ hours, or until tender, turning frequently and adding a little more water, if necessary. Serve on a platter surrounded by sautéed mushrooms and parsley potatoes.

Serves 8-10.

VEAU À L'ALSACIENNE

BRAISED STUFFED VEAL

4-pound leg of veal, boned
Salt, freshly ground black pepper
2 tablespoons butter
1 large onion, chopped
¾ cup dry bread crumbs
⅓ cup heavy cream
1 tablespoon chopped parsley
2 eggs, beaten
2 cups dry white wine
2 cups water
2 carrots, sliced
1 onion, sliced
Bouquet garni (or bay leaf, sprig parsley, and stalk celery, tied together)
1 tablespoon flour

Flatten the boned veal and season inside with salt and pepper. Melt 1 tablespoon butter in a skillet and sauté the onion 5 minutes. Combine the bread crumbs moistened with the cream, the sautéed onion, parsley, beaten eggs, and salt and pepper to taste. Spread veal with this stuffing, roll up and tie securely. Sew edges together to keep stuffing from leaking out. Put veal in a deep pan and pour in the wine and water. Add sliced carrots and onion, bouquet garni, and salt and pepper to taste. Cover pan and braise veal over low heat for 2 hours, or until tender, turning meat when it is half cooked.

Transfer veal to a hot platter; remove bouquet garni. Purée the sauce and vegetables for a few seconds in an electric blender, or strain sauce into a saucepan. There should be about 2 cups.

Blend together the remaining tablespoon butter and the flour. Put the saucepan over medium heat and stir in the butter-flour mixture. Cook a little to thicken. Serve sauce separately.

Serves 6-8.

VEAU FARCI

Stuffed Breast of Veal

Breast of veal, boned, with pocket for stuffing
4 teaspoons salt
¾ teaspoon freshly ground black pepper
4 tablespoons butter
1 cup chopped onions
¼ pound mushrooms, sliced
¾ cup fresh bread crumbs
2 beaten eggs
¼ cup heavy cream
1 tablespoon minced parsley
2 carrots, sliced
1 onion, sliced
1 bay leaf
½ teaspoon thyme
1 cup dry red wine
1 cup boiling water

Season the veal inside and out with 2½ teaspoons salt and ½ teaspoon pepper.

Melt 2 tablespoons butter in a skillet and sauté the chopped onions 5 minutes. Add the mushrooms and sauté 5 minutes. Stir in the bread crumbs, eggs, cream, parsley, and remaining salt and pepper and mix well together. Stuff the veal with this mixture and sew or skewer the openings.

Melt the remaining butter in a Dutch oven or covered roasting pan and brown the veal all over. Add to the pan the carrots, sliced onion, bay leaf, thyme, wine, and water. Cover and cook over low heat 2½ hours, or until tender, turning the meat once or twice. Remove veal to a hot serving platter. Discard bay leaf and purée the juices and vegetables in an electric blender or rub through a sieve. Thicken the sauce if necessary with a little flour mixed with cold water. Adjust seasoning and serve separately.

Serves 6-8.

VEAU FARCI AUX FOIES DE VOLAILLE

Veal with Liver Stuffing

Breast of veal, boned, with pocket for stuffing
4 teaspoons salt
¾ teaspoon freshly ground black pepper
4 tablespoons butter
½ pound mushrooms, chopped
¾ pound raw chicken livers, chopped
¼ cup chopped onions
3 tablespoons dry bread crumbs
2 tablespoons dry red wine
1 beaten egg
¼ teaspoon marjoram
¼ teaspoon thyme
2 onions
3 cloves
2 cups chicken stock
1 cup dry red wine

Season the veal with 3 teaspoons salt and ½ teaspoon pepper. Melt 2 tablespoons butter in a skillet and sauté the mushrooms 5 minutes. Mix in the livers, chopped onions, bread crumbs, 2 tablespoons wine, egg, marjoram, thyme, and the remaining salt and pepper. Stuff the veal with this mixture and sew or skewer the openings.

Melt the remaining butter in a Dutch oven and brown the veal on all sides. Stick the onions with the cloves and add to the pan with the stock and wine. Cover and cook over low heat 2½ hours or until tender, turning the meat frequently. Adjust seasoning.

Serves 8-10.

ÉTUVÉE DE VEAU

Veal in Red Wine

2 tablespoons butter
20 small white onions
20 small cubes lean bacon
2 pounds veal, cut in 1½-inch cubes
Salt, freshly ground black pepper
Bouquet garni (or bay leaf, sprig parsley, and piece celery, tied together)
2 cloves garlic
2½ cups dry red wine
1 tablespoon potato flour

Melt the butter in a heavy pan and sauté the onions and bacon cubes until onions are slightly browned. Remove onions and bacon, add veal to pan, and brown on all sides. Season with salt and pepper and add the bay leaf, parsley, celery, garlic, and wine. Replace onions and bacon, cover, and cook over low heat 2 hours. Mix potato starch with a little water or red wine and stir into the liquid. Simmer 15 minutes. Remove bay leaf, parsley, celery, and garlic. It is essential to have the right amount of liquid, neither too little nor too much. If the juices cook down too much, add a little hot water. If there is too much liquid left when the meat is tender, strain it off and reduce quickly over high heat.

Serves 4-6.

BLANQUETTE DE VEAU

Fricassee of Veal

3 pounds boneless veal
1 carrot, quartered
2 onions
1 bay leaf
1½ teaspoons salt
¼ teaspoon freshly ground white pepper
½ teaspoon thyme
2 tablespoons butter
2 tablespoons flour
2 egg yolks
¼ cup light cream
1 cup sliced sautéed mushrooms

Cut the veal into oblongs about 2 inches by 5 inches and 1 inch thick. Put in a saucepan with cold water to cover and bring to a boil. Skim the surface of the liquid and add the carrot, onions, bay leaf, salt, pepper, and thyme. Cover and cook over medium heat 1 hour or until veal is tender. Remove meat. Strain the stock, reserving 2½ cups.

Melt the butter in a saucepan, stir in the flour. When smooth, slowly mix in the reserved stock and stir steadily to the boiling point. Cook over low heat 10 minutes. Beat the egg yolks and cream in a bowl and slowly mix in a little hot sauce, stirring constantly to prevent curdling. Mix into sauce in pan and cook, stirring with a whisk, until thickened. Mix in the veal and mushrooms and correct seasoning. Cook over very low heat for 10 minutes, but do not allow to boil.

Serves 4-6.

FRICASSÉE DE VEAU À L'ANCIENNE

Fricassee of Veal in the Old Style

1 carrot
1 onion
Bouquet garni (or 1 bay leaf, sprig parsley, and stalk celery, tied together)
3 cups water
¾ teaspoon salt
¼ teaspoon freshly ground black pepper
2 pounds lean veal, cut into large cubes
2 tablespoons diced salt pork
1 tablespoon butter
1 onion, chopped
1 tablespoon flour
½ cup dry white wine
12 small white onions
8 mushrooms
2 egg yolks
½ cup cream
Finely chopped parsley and chives

Make a court-bouillon by simmering the carrot, onion, bouquet garni, water, and salt and pepper for 20 minutes. Add the veal and parboil 5 minutes (the meat should be covered but there should not be an excessive amount of water). Remove meat. Reserve court-bouillon. Blanch the salt pork in boiling water for 1 minute. Drain. Put in a saucepan with the butter and chopped onion. Cook onion 5 minutes, but do not brown. Add veal and stir in flour, white wine, and the reserved court-bouillon. Cover and simmer 2 hours, or until tender, adding the small white onions and mushrooms ½ hour before serving. Remove bouquet garni. Beat the egg yolks with the cream in a bowl; add a little hot sauce to egg-cream mixture, stirring steadily to prevent curdling. Return to balance of sauce. Reheat but do not boil. Adjust seasoning, sprinkle with chopped parsley and chives, and serve.

Serves 4.

VEAU À LA MONTSOREAU

Veal, Montsoreau Style

2 pieces fresh pork rind
2 onions, sliced
2 carrots, sliced
Bouquet garni (or bay leaf, sprig parsley, and piece celery, tied together)
4-pound rolled roast of veal
Salt, freshly ground black pepper
½ cup dry white wine
3 cups veal or chicken stock

Spread the pork rind, onions, and carrots over the bottom of an earthenware casserole. Add the bouquet garni. Put the veal on top and roast in a 350° oven 25 minutes. Season with salt and pepper to taste and add the wine and ½ cup stock. Continue roasting until liquid has almost completely reduced and then add the remaining stock. Reduce heat to 275°, cover and braise for 2½ hours or until thoroughly cooked and almost tender enough to cut with a spoon. Transfer to a hot serving platter. Serve with Onion Purée and a sauce made by reducing the pan juices until syrupy.

Serves 6-8.

CÔTELETTES DE VEAU EN CASSEROLE

Casserole of Veal Chops

6 loin veal chops, 1 inch thick
1½ teaspoons salt
¼ teaspoon freshly ground black pepper
6 tablespoons butter
1 cup dry bread crumbs
2 cloves
6 small white onions
1 clove garlic, minced
½ pound mushrooms, sliced
3 cups beef stock
1 cup dry white wine
1 bay leaf
¼ teaspoon thyme
2 tablespoons minced parsley

Season the chops with salt and pepper. Melt the butter in a casserole and brown the chops on both sides. Remove. Stir bread crumbs into butter and brown. Return chops to the casserole. Stick the cloves in one onion and add to the casserole the onions, garlic, mushrooms, stock, wine, bay leaf, and thyme. Cover and cook in a 375° oven for 1 hour, removing the cover for the last 15 minutes. Sprinkle top with parsley and serve.

Serves 6.

GIGOT D'AGNEAU À LA BRETONNE

Roast Lamb with Beans

2 cups dried white beans or green flageolets
1 onion
5 cloves garlic
1 bay leaf
½ teaspoon thyme
¼ teaspoon marjoram
1 cup skinned, chopped tomatoes
2 tablespoons butter
1 tablespoon salt
¾ teaspoon freshly ground black pepper
5- to 6-pound leg of lamb

Wash the beans, cover with cold water, and bring to a boil. Remove from heat and let stand to soak 1 hour. Drain. Cover with fresh water and add the onion, 2 cloves garlic, bay leaf, thyme, and marjoram. Cook 1½ hours or until tender but firm. Discard onion, garlic, and bay leaf. Put beans in a casserole and mix with the tomatoes, butter, and some of the salt and pepper.

While the beans are cooking, mince the remaining garlic, mix with most of the salt and pepper, prick the lamb all over, and rub with the mixture. Place in a shallow roasting pan and roast in a 425° oven 30 minutes, turning to brown evenly. Reduce heat to 350° and roast 1¼ hours longer. The lamb should still be pink inside.

Add 4 tablespoons of the lamb juices to the beans and serve as an accompaniment to the roast lamb.

Serves 8-10.

DAUBE À LA MODE D'AVIGNON

Lamb in Red Wine

2 cups dry red wine
2 cloves garlic, minced
1 cup sliced onions
2 bay leaves
3 peppercorns
½ teaspoon thyme
3 pounds boneless lamb, cut in 1½-inch cubes
3 slices salt pork, diced
1½ teaspoons salt
½ teaspoon freshly ground black pepper
1 cup skinned, diced tomatoes
3 tablespoons minced parsley

Combine the wine, garlic, onions, bay leaves, peppercorns, and thyme in a glass or pottery bowl, add the lamb, and marinate overnight.

Brown the salt pork in an earthenware casserole (if you do not have one, use a regular casserole or Dutch oven) and pour off the fat. Drain the lamb, reserving the marinade, and season with the salt and pepper. Add to casserole and cook over medium heat 10 minutes. Add reserved marinade, tomatoes, and parsley, cover tightly, and cook in a 300° oven 3 hours. Skim fat off top, adjust seasoning, and serve.

Serves 6-8.

NAVARIN DE MOUTON

Lamb Stew

2 tablespoons lard or bacon fat
8 small white onions
3 pounds shoulder of lamb, cut into cubes
1 teaspoon salt
¼ teaspoon freshly ground black pepper
1 tablespoon flour
¾ cup beef stock
½ cup dry white wine
1 clove garlic
Bouquet garni (bay leaf, parsley, and celery, tied together)
6 potatoes, peeled and quartered
Chopped parsley

Melt the lard in a heavy pan, add the onions, lamb, salt and pepper. Brown onions and lamb all over. Pour off most of the fat and blend in the flour. Gradually add the stock and wine, stirring to the boiling point. Add garlic, bouquet garni, and enough hot water to cover. Cover pan and simmer over very low heat 1 hour, or until lamb is tender. After lamb has cooked ½ hour, add potatoes and continue cooking. taste for seasoning. Before serving, remove garlic and bouquet garni. Serve the stew in a deep hot dish and sprinkle with parsley.

Serves 6.

RAGOÛT DE MOUTON

Lamb Ragout

3 pounds shoulder or breast of lamb
3 tablespoons butter
3 tablespoons flour
4 cups water
12 small white onions
4 carrots
3 sprigs parsley
1 bay leaf
2 teaspoons salt
¼ teaspoon freshly ground black pepper
¼ teaspoon thyme
6 potatoes, peeled and quartered
1 pound green peas, shelled or 1 package frozen, thawed
2 tablespoons chopped parsley

Cut the lamb in small pieces. Heat the butter in a heavy pan or Dutch oven and brown the lamb on all sides. Stir in the flour until browned. Add the water, stirring to the boiling point. Add the onions, carrots, parsley, bay leaf, salt, pepper, and thyme. Cover and cook over low heat 1¼ hours. Add the potatoes and peas and cook 45 minutes longer. Discard parsley and bay leaf. Serve in a deep platter, sprinkled with parsley.

Serves 6-8.

RESTES DE GIGOT À LA BRISSAC

Lamb in White Wine Sauce

2 tablespoons butter
8 slices roast lamb (leftovers)
2 tablespoons chopped onions
1 teaspoon chopped parsley
2 tablespoons flour
½ cup dry white wine
¼ cup water
2 tablespoons olive oil
1 teaspoon salt
¼ teaspoon freshly ground black pepper

Melt the butter in a skillet and brown the lamb slices, turning once. Add onions and parsley and sauté 5 minutes. Stir in the flour until browned. Add the wine and water, stirring to the boiling point. Cover and cook over medium heat 30 minutes. Add olive oil, salt and pepper, and cook 10 minutes longer. Check seasoning. Serve with boiled potatoes or boiled rice.

Serves 4-8.

RAGOÛT D'AGNEAU

Lamb Casserole

3 pounds boneless lamb
3 tablespoons olive oil
¼ pound ham, diced
¾ cup chopped onions
1½ teaspoons salt
½ teaspoon freshly ground black pepper
Dash ground allspice
1 bay leaf
1½ cups beef stock
2 cups diced potatoes
2 cups shelled green peas or 1 package frozen, thawed

Cut the lamb in 1½-inch cubes. Heat the oil in a heavy casserole, add the lamb and ham, and brown. Mix in the onions and continue browning. Season with the salt, pepper, and allspice; add the bay leaf and stock. Cover and cook over low heat 45 minutes. Add the potatoes and peas, cover, and cook 25 minutes. Correct seasoning.

Serves 6-8.

CÔTELETTES DE PORC À LA COURLANDAISE

PORK CHOPS WITH CHESTNUTS AND RED CABBAGE

6 loin pork chops, 1½ inches thick
1 egg, beaten
2 tablespoons butter
2 tablespoons flour
2 teaspoons salt
¼ teaspoon freshly ground black pepper
1 cup chicken stock
1 teaspoon lemon juice
2 teaspoons chopped parsley
1 pound chestnuts, cooked and peeled
1 3-pound head red cabbage, coarsely shredded
1 cup water

Dip the chops in the egg. Heat the butter in a heavy skillet and brown the chops for 5 minutes on each side. Cover and cook over low heat 20 minutes. Remove chops and keep warm. Mix the flour into the pan and season with 1 teaspoon salt and the pepper. Add the stock, stirring to the boiling point. Reduce heat and simmer 10 minutes. Mix in the lemon juice and parsley.

While the chops are cooking, combine the chestnuts and cabbage in a saucepan. Add the water and remaining salt and cook 15 minutes. Drain well. Arrauge chops in the center of a hot serving platter and surround with the cabbage and chestnuts. Serve sauce separately.

Serves 6.

CASSOULET

Mixed Meat and Bean Casserole

4 cups dried pea beans
2 onions, stuck with 2 cloves
2 cloves garlic, minced
⅛ pound salt pork, diced
1 bay leaf
½ teaspoon thyme
2 tablespoons salad oil
1½ pounds pork, cubed
1 pound lamb, cubed
1½ cups chopped onions
1 6-ounce can tomato sauce
1 cup dry white wine
1 tablespoon salt
2 garlic sausages
1 roast duck

Wash beans, cover with water, and bring to a boil. Cook 2 minutes. Remove from heat and allow to stand 1 hour. Drain. Put in a deep pan with 2 quarts water, the onions, garlic, salt pork, bay leaf, and thyme and bring to a boil. Reduce heat and cook over medium heat 1 hour.

Meanwhile, heat the oil in a skillet and brown the lamb and pork on all sides. Remove. Add onions to skillet and brown. Add browned meats, onions, tomato sauce, wine, and salt to beans, cover, and cook over low heat 1 hour. Transfer to a large casserole. Slice the sausages and cut meat from bones of duck. Lightly mix them into the beans. Correct seasoning and bake in a 350° oven 40 minutes.

Note: Confit d'oie (preserved goose) is traditionally used in place of duck and is a notable addition. It is available in cans.

Serves 8-10.

CASSOULET DE CASTELNAUDARY

Bean Casserole with Meat

2 pounds dried white beans
5 quarts water
½ pound pork rind
¼ pound bacon or salt ham
6 cloves garlic, chopped
1 sprig thyme or ¼ teaspoon dried
2 tablespoons salt
½ teaspoon freshly ground black pepper
1 pound fresh sausages
2 pounds fresh pork, cut in 1-ounce cubes
Confit d'oie (*preserved goose, available in cans*) *or ½ roast duck*

Soak beans in tepid water 2 hours. Drain. Put in a large kettle with the water, pork rind, bacon or ham, garlic, thyme, salt and pepper. Gradually bring to a boil and simmer over very low heat 1½ hours or until tender. Do not let boil or bean skins will break.

Meanwhile, broil the sausage and brown the pork cubes in goose fat (from the *confit d'oie*) or other fat. Add 2 tablespoons hot water to pan, rinse out juices and add to beans. When the beans are cooked, remove pork rind and bacon and cut into ¾-inch squares.

You will need a casserole (large earthenware pot) for the cassoulet. Put ⅓ of the beans in the bottom and place in the center of the beans a leg and second joint of the *confit d'oie,* or the duck, cut up. Surround it with the pork cubes, sausages, and squares of pork rind and bacon. Cover with remaining beans and their juices. Put in a 225° oven and bake 4 hours or longer. It must be as low a temperature as possible so the dish is quite liquid and delicious.

Serves 8-10.

TOURTE LORRAINE

Meat Pie, Lorraine Fashion

½ pound lean pork, finely diced
½ pound veal, finely diced
1 clove garlic, chopped
1 shallot, chopped
1 teaspoon chopped parsley
1 cup dry white wine
Salt, freshly ground black pepper
Puff Paste or Flaky Pastry (see recipes)
3 eggs, beaten
2 cups cream

Marinate the pork and veal in a mixture of the garlic, shallot, parsley, wine, and salt and pepper to taste, for 24 hours.

Line a round, deep pie dish with some of the pastry. Remove meats from marinade, drain and dry well, and put in pie dish. Cover with pastry and seal the edges. Cut a small hole in the center of the pastry. Bake the pie in a preheated 425° oven 25 minutes.

Mix the eggs and cream, and season with a little salt. Insert a small funnel in the hole in the pie crust and pour in the egg-cream mixture, a little at a time. Reduce heat to 325° and bake 20 minutes more. Serve hot.

Serves 3-4.

CÔTES DE PORC AUX PRUNEAUX

Pork Chops with Prunes

18 unsweetened prunes
½ cup port
½ cup water
6 pork chops, ¾ inch thick
1½ teaspoons salt
¼ teaspoon freshly ground black pepper
¼ cup flour
2 tablespoons butter
2 tablespoons brandy
2 tablespoons heavy cream

Soak the prunes in hot water 15 minutes. Drain. Put in a pan with the port and water and cook until tender but firm.

Season the chops with the salt and pepper and dust with the flour. Melt the butter in a skillet and sauté the chops until the meat is white and the chops browned on the outside, about 30 minutes. Remove chops to a hot serving platter.

Drain the prunes, reserving ½ cup liquid, and arrange them around the chops. Add the brandy to the skillet juices, warm and flame. When flames subside, mix the prune liquid and the cream into the skillet and cook over high heat 1 minute, scraping the glaze from the pan. Pour over chops.

Serves 6.

JAMBON AU CHAMPAGNE

Ham with Champagne Sauce

12-pound ham
2 beaten eggs
1 cup brown sugar
1 can sliced pineapple
1½ cups champagne
2 tablespoons butter

Cook the ham according to the package directions and drain well. Score the fat in a diamond design, brush with the egg, and spread with the sugar. Drain the pineapple and reserve ¾ cup juice. Put ham in a roasting pan and pour the pineapple juice and champagne around it. Bake in a 375° oven 1 hour, basting frequently so the ham gets a good glaze. Remove ham to a hot serving platter. Skim fat from the pan juices.

Melt the butter in a skillet and lightly brown the pineapple slices on both sides. Arrange around the ham. Serve the gravy separately.

Serves 12-16.

JAMBON NIVERNAIS

Ham Nivernais

1 tablespoon sweet butter
4 slices cooked ham
½ cup dry white wine
Flour
½ cup chicken or veal stock
¼ cup heavy cream

Melt the butter in a skillet, add the ham slices, and brown lightly on each side. Add wine and reduce to half. Transfer ham to a hot serving dish. Sprinkle a little flour into the pan and blend; gradually add the stock, stirring to the boiling point. Simmer 5 minutes, stir in cream, and pour sauce over ham.

Serves 4.

LE SAUPIQUET NIVERNAIS

Ham in Wine Sauce

5 tablespoons butter
12 thin slices cooked ham
1 tablespoon flour
¼ teaspoon salt
Freshly ground white pepper
¾ cup consommé
¼ cup dry white wine
¼ cup wine vinegar
2 shallots, finely chopped
6 juniper berries (optional)
Heavy cream
Chopped parsley

Melt 4 tablespoons butter in a skillet and sauté the ham for a few minutes on each side. Transfer to a hot serving platter.

Brown the flour slightly in a hot saucepan. Stir in the remaining butter, salt, and a little pepper and gradually stir in the consommé, wine, and vinegar. Add the shallots and juniper berries and stir to the boiling point. Simmer for 10 minutes or until fairly thick. Strain sauce through a very fine sieve. Measure and add ¼ of its volume in heavy cream.

Pour sauce over ham slices, sprinkle with a little chopped parsley, and serve.

Serves 4.

LANGUE DE BOEUF BRAISÉE

Braised Tongue

5-pound fresh beef tongue
2 tablespoons butter
1½ cups sliced onions
1 cup sliced carrots
2 cups dry white wine
2 tablespoons flour
3 cups beef stock
3 sprigs parsley
2 stalks celery
2 tomatoes, skinned and diced
1 bay leaf
1½ teaspoons salt
½ teaspoon freshly ground black pepper
½ teaspoon thyme

Wash the tongue and trim the root end. Put in a pan, cover with water, and bring to a boil. Cook 5 minutes. Drain and peel off skin.

Melt the butter in a Dutch oven and brown the tongue, onions, and carrots. Pour off the fat. Stir in the wine and cook over low heat 15 minutes. Mix the flour with the stock and slowly add to the pan, stirring until thickened. Tie together the parsley and celery. Put in the pan with the tomatoes, bay leaf, salt, pepper, and thyme. Cover and cook over low heat 2¾ hours or until tongue is tender. Adjust seasoning. Remove tongue, put on a serving platter, and cut as many slices as needed. Strain the gravy and serve separately.

Serves 8-10.

FOIE DE VEAU À LA BOURGEOISE

Calf's Liver, Family Style

2 pounds calf's liver, in one piece
6 small strips salt pork or bacon
2 tablespoons butter
2 tablespoons flour
½ cup water
½ cup white wine
2 cloves
1 bay leaf
¾ teaspoon salt
½ teaspoon freshly ground black pepper
12 small white onions, cooked 10 minutes
8 carrots, cut in small pieces, cooked 10 minutes
Parsley sprigs

Pierce the surface of the liver on the side with the point of a sharp knife and insert the salt pork strips. Heat butter in a heavy ovenproof casserole and brown liver on both sides. Remove from pan. Mix in flour until browned. Add the water and wine, stirring to the boiling point. Add cloves, bay leaf, salt, pepper, liver, onions, and carrots. Cover casserole and cook in a 300° oven 1 hour. Transfer liver to a hot serving platter and surround with onions and carrots. Strain the sauce. If too thin, thicken with a little potato starch or cornstarch mixed to a paste with cold water. Stir into sauce and simmer just until thickened. Pour sauce over liver and garnish with parsley.

Serves 4-6.

RIS DE VEAU

Parboiled Sweetbreads

3 pairs sweetbreads
4 cups water
1 teaspoon salt
1 tablespoon vinegar

Wash the sweetbreads and soak in ice water for 1 hour. Drain and add the 4 cups water, the salt, and vinegar. Bring to a boil and cook over low heat 10 minutes. Drain and cover with fresh cold water until cool. Drain again. Remove the membranes and connective tissues. Always keep refrigerated until ready to use, as they spoil quickly. Use as directed in recipes.

RIS DE VEAU À LA LYONNAISE

Sweetbreads in Herb Sauce

3 pairs parboiled sweetbreads (see recipe)
4 tablespoons butter
1 clove garlic, minced
2 teaspoons minced parsley
2 teaspoons chopped chives or green onions
½ teaspoon salt
⅛ teaspoon freshly ground white pepper
½ teaspoon tarragon
1¼ cups chicken stock
1 egg yolk
1 teaspoon lemon juice

Halve the sweetbreads lengthwise and then cut in quarters crosswise. Melt the butter in a skillet and lightly brown the sweetbreads on both sides. Sprinkle with the garlic, parsley, chives, salt, pepper, and tarragon and mix in the chicken stock. Bring to a boil and cook over low heat 5 minutes.

Beat the egg yolk and lemon juice in a bowl and mix in a little of the hot sauce, stirring steadily to prevent curdling. Return to skillet and heat but do not allow to boil. Correct seasoning. Serve in patty shells or croustade.

Serves 6.

RIS DE VEAU À L'OIGNON

Sweetbreads, Lyonnaise Style

1 pair parboiled sweetbreads
2 tablespoons butter
1 onion, finely chopped
1 clove garlic, finely chopped
1 carrot, finely chopped
1 bay leaf
Pinch of thyme
½ cup white wine
½ cup veal or chicken stock
Onion purée (see recipe)
2 teaspoons flour
3 mushrooms, sautéed and sliced
¼ cup diced ham
Grated Swiss cheese

Put sweetbreads between two plates with a weight on top and cool. Heat butter in a large saucepan, add onion, garlic, carrot, bay leaf, thyme, and sweetbreads. Sauté sweetbreads 5 minutes on each side. Stir in wine and stock, cover, and simmer gently 5 minutes. Remove and slice sweetbreads and keep warm. Strain sauce into another pan and mix in the onion purée. Arrange sweetbreads on a serving dish and put on top of them the sliced mushrooms and diced ham. Cover with sauce, sprinkle with cheese, dot with butter, and brown lightly in a 425° oven.

Serves 2.

ROGNONS DE VEAU FLAMBÉS

Veal Kidneys in Cognac

4 veal kidneys
4 tablespoons butter
¾ cup sliced mushrooms
½ cup cognac
⅛ teaspoon dry mustard
1½ teaspoons salt
¼ teaspoon freshly ground black pepper
¼ cup heavy cream

Wash the kidneys and soak in cold water 1 hour. Remove white core and slice each kidney in four.

Melt 2 tablespoons butter in a skillet and sauté the mushrooms 5 minutes. Remove. Melt remaining butter and sauté kidneys 2 minutes on each side. Warm the cognac and flame the kidneys. When flames die, add mushrooms to pan and season with the mustard, salt, and pepper. Cook 1 minute. Stir in the cream and heat through but do not boil.

Serves 4.

RAGOÛT DE QUEUE DE BOEUF

Oxtail Stew

2 2-pound oxtails, cut in serving-sized pieces
¾ cup flour
2 teaspoons salt
½ teaspoon freshly ground black pepper
½ teaspoon powdered thyme
4 tablespoons olive oil
2 cups boiling water
3 cups dry red wine
2 cloves
12 small white onions
3 sprigs parsley
2 stalks celery
1 bay leaf
1 clove garlic, minced
1 leek
3 carrots, sliced in eighths lengthwise
4 potatoes, peeled and diced
1 cup sliced mushrooms

Roll the oxtail pieces in a mixture of the flour, salt, pepper, and thyme. Heat the oil in a deep heavy casserole or Dutch oven and brown the oxtails on all sides. Pour off the fat. Add to the casserole the boiling water and wine. Stick the cloves in one of the onions, and tie the parsley and celery together. Add to the casserole all the onions, the parsley-celery bundle, the bay leaf, garlic, and leek. Cover tightly and cook in a 300° oven 2½ hours. Add the carrots, potatoes, and mushrooms. Cover and bake 1 hour. Skim fat off the top, adjust seasoning, and serve in the casserole.

Serves 6-8.

TRIPES À LA MODE DE CAEN

Tripe, Caen Fashion

4 pounds honeycomb tripe
3 thin slices salt pork
2 cups sliced onions
2 carrots, sliced
3 stalks celery, thinly sliced
1 green pepper, chopped
2 calf's feet, cut up
2 bay leaves
2 teaspoons salt
½ teaspoon freshly ground black pepper
¼ teaspoon thyme
¼ teaspoon marjoram
2 sprigs parsley
4 cups beef stock
4 cups cider
½ cup tomato paste
¼ cup Calvados or apple brandy

This dish should be started a day before you want to serve it, as it requires long slow cooking.

Wash the tripe under running water, then soak in water to cover 1 hour, changing the water three times. Drain. Cut tripe in narrow strips, 3 inches long.

Place the salt pork on the bottom of a Dutch oven or heavy earthenware pot with a tight-fitting lid. Arrange on top of the pork the onions, carrots, celery, and green pepper. On top of the vegetables put the tripe and calf's feet, sprinkle with the bay leaves, salt, pepper, thyme, marjoram, and parsley, and pour on the stock and cider, adding a little more if the liquid doesn't cover the mixture. Cover tightly and wrap aluminum foil around the edge of the cover to keep the steam from escpaing. Cook in a 225° oven for 15 hours (most of the cooking may be done overnight). Remove from oven, put pan on direct heat, stir in the tomato paste and apple brandy, and cook 30 minutes. Correct seasoning. Serve in deep bowls. This dish tastes even better when reheated.

Serves 6-8.

Vegetables and Salads

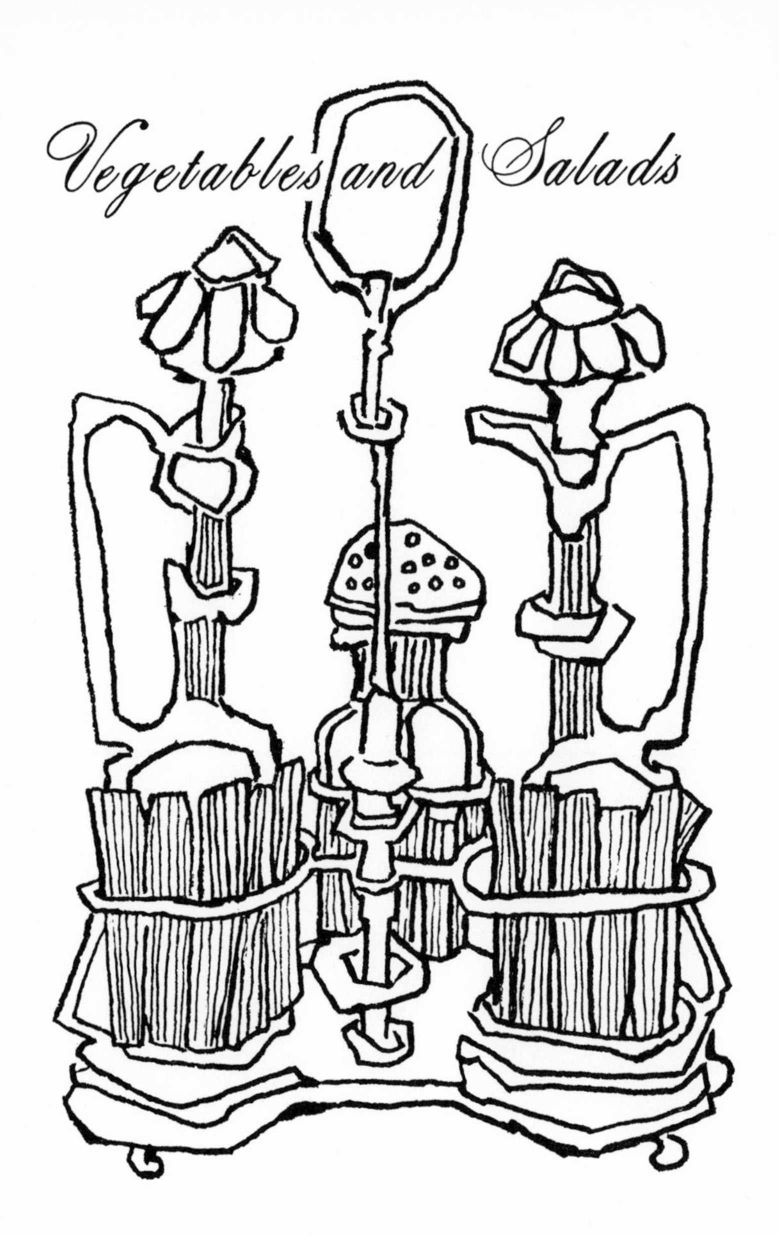

Vegetables and Salads

ARTICHAUTS À LA BARIGOULE

Stuffed Artichokes

4 medium-sized artichokes
1 cup dry bread crumbs
½ cup chicken stock
¼ pound sausage meat
1 small onion, finely chopped
2 tablespoons chopped parsley
¼ pound mushrooms, finely chopped
2 tablespoons butter
1 tablespoon flour
¾ teaspoon salt
¼ teaspoon freshly ground black pepper
1 tablespoon oil
4 slices lemon

Slice off the stem and the top of the artichokes and remove the hard outer leaves. Plunge, stem end down, into rapidly boiling salted water and boil uncovered 30 minutes, or until outer leaves can be detached easily. Drain and turn upside down, pressing to remove water. Cut out the chokes (furry centers).

Mix the bread crumbs and stock and combine with the sausage meat, onion, parsley, and mushrooms. Melt the butter in a skillet and sauté the mixture until it is light brown. Blend in the flour until smooth, then season with the salt and pepper. Stuff centers of each artichoke with this mixture. Heat a casserole big enough to hold the artichokes and brush the inside with the oil. Arrange the artichokes in it and bake in a 350° oven 30 minutes. Serve with lemon slices.

Serves 4.

ASPERGES NORMANDES

Asparagus with Cider Sauce

1 bunch asparagus
1 tablespoon butter
2 teaspoons flour
1 teaspoon salt
¼ teaspoon freshly ground black pepper
⅛ teaspoon grated nutmeg
⅓ cup cider
⅔ cup heavy cream
Lemon juice

Steam the asparagus in a double boiler with the top inverted. Place only the stalks in the boiling water, leaving the few inches of the tips out of the water. Cook until tender but still firm.

Meanwhile, melt the butter in a saucepan, blend in the flour, and season with salt, pepper, and grated nutmeg. Stirring constantly, gradually add cider and cream and simmer just until thickened. Place sauce over boiling water and cook for 10 minutes. Add a few drops of lemon juice and pour over asparagus. Other vegetables such as cooked cauliflower, carrots, celery, leeks, can also be served with this sauce. These asparagus are best served as a separate course.

Serves 4.

HARICOTS VERTS À LA NIÇOISE

Green Beans in Tomato Sauce

¼ cup olive oil
1 clove garlic, minced
1 cup chopped onions
¼ cup diced green peppers
2 cups canned tomatoes
1 bay leaf
2 tablespoons minced parsley
¼ teaspoon sugar
2 teaspoons salt
¼ teaspoon freshly ground black pepper
1½ pounds cut green beans or 2 packages frozen, thawed

Heat the oil in a saucepan, add the garlic, onions, and green peppers and sauté 5 minutes. Add the tomatoes, bay leaf, parsley, sugar, salt and pepper, bring to a boil, and cook over low heat 15 minutes. Stir in the beans, cover, and cook over low heat 25 minutes. Season to taste.

Serves 6.

HARICOTS VERTS À LA LYONNAISE

Sautéed Green Beans with Onions

1½ pounds green beans or 2 packages frozen
¾ cup chopped onions
4 tablespoons butter
1½ teaspoons salt
⅛ teaspoon freshly ground white pepper
⅛ teaspoon tarragon or wine vinegar
2 tablespoons minced parsley

Cook the beans in salted water until tender but still firm. Drain well. Sauté the onions in the butter until soft and transparent. Mix in the beans, salt and pepper, and sauté 5 minutes. Sprinkle with the vinegar and parsley.

Serves 6.

CHOU FARCI

Stuffed Cabbage

1 large firm cabbage
½ pound sausage meat
½ pound beef or veal, ground
1 teaspoon salt
¼ teaspoon freshly ground black pepper
2 tablespoons butter
2 tablespoons flour
2 cups beef stock or water
1 onion, thinly sliced
1 carrot, cut in rounds
1 veal knuckle or soupbone, sawed in 2 or 3 pieces

Remove the tough outer leaves of cabbage and cut out center core carefully and discard. Pour boiling water over it. Drain well.

Mix together the sausage meat and chopped beef or veal; season with the salt and pepper. Put a little of this mixture between each cabbage leaf, starting from the center and working out. Stuff the center. Reshape cabbage and tie firmly with string.

Melt the butter in a pan large and deep enough to hold the cabbage. Stir in the flour until browned. Mix in the stock or water, stirring to the boiling point. Carefully place cabbage in pan and add onion, carrot, and veal knuckle. Cover tightly and simmer 2 hours, adding more liquid if needed. Transfer cabbage to a deep serving dish and remove string. Strain sauce and pour over cabbage. Cut into wedges.

Serves 4.

CHOU ROUGE AUX POMMES

Red Cabbage with Apples

1 3-pound red cabbage
3 large apples, peeled and sliced
2 tablespoons butter
3 cloves
1½ teaspoons salt
¼ teaspoon freshly ground black pepper
1 teaspoon cornstarch
1 tablespoon cider vinegar
2 tablespoons currant jelly

Discard the outer leaves of the cabbage; wash, and shred the cabbage coarsely and put in a large pan of water, to cover. Add the apples, butter, cloves, salt and pepper. Cover pan and simmer 2 hours. Mix together the cornstarch, vinegar, and jelly and stir into the sauce, until thickened. Serve very hot.

Serves 4-6.

CHOUX ROUGES À LA FLAMANDE

Red Cabbage in Red Wine

2 2-pound firm heads red cabbage
4 tablespoons butter
4 apples (preferably tart), peeled and quartered
1 onion, chopped
1½ teaspoons salt
¼ teaspoon freshly ground pepper
2 cloves
1 bay leaf
2 tablespoons wine vinegar
1½ cups dry red wine
2 tablespoons brown sugar

Wash cabbage well, dry, and slice finely, discarding thick center stem. Melt 2 tablespoons butter in a heavy pan or Dutch oven and put in the cabbage, apples, onion, salt, pepper, cloves, bay leaf, vinegar, and red wine. Bring to a boil, cover, and simmer over low heat 3 hours, adding a little hot water during cooking if necessary. Stir in brown sugar and mix in remaining butter; cook 5 minutes. Remove bay leaf and cloves. Serve in a deep dish.

Serves 6-8.

CAROTTES AU SUCRE

Glazed Carrots

1 bunch young carrots, cut in small, even pieces
2 tablespoons butter
Salt
1 teaspoon sugar

Put carrots in a shallow pan and barely cover with water. Add butter, salt to taste, and sugar. Stir and cook gently until water has evaporated and carrots are lightly glazed.

Serves 4.

CÉLERIS À LA BONNE FEMME

Celery Bonne Femme

2 bunches celery
2 tablespoons butter
½ cup chopped onions
1 carrot, grated
½ cup beef stock
1 cup skinned, diced tomatoes
1 bay leaf
1 teaspoon salt
⅛ teaspoon freshly ground black pepper
2 tablespoons minced parsley

Trim off celery leaves and cut bunches in half lengthwise and then across in 2-inch pieces.

Melt the butter in a saucepan and sauté the onions and carrot until browned. Mix in the celery and cook 3 minutes, stirring frequently. Add the stock, tomatoes, bay leaf, salt and pepper, cover, and cook 45 minutes over low heat. Discard bay leaf, adjust seasoning, and sprinkle with parsley.

Serves 6.

CÉLERI-RAVE EN TIMBALE

Baked Celery Root

3 celery roots (celeriac), cleaned and peeled
3 tablespoons butter
2 to 3 tablespoons stock
2 egg yolks

Cut 2 of the celeriac into pieces and blanch 5 minutes in boiling water. Cook until soft in 2 tablespoons butter, then mash and purée in an electric blender or by forcing through a sieve. Finely dice the remaining celeriac and sauté in the remaining butter. Add stock and cook until absorbed. Mix together the puréed and the diced celeriac and blend in the egg yolks. Fill small buttered ramekins with the mixture, place in a pan containing a little hot water, and bake in a

250° oven about 20 minutes or until firm to the touch. Unmold.

Serves 6-8.

AUBERGINES À LA BORDELAISE

Sautéed Eggplant

1 eggplant
2 teaspoons salt
4 tablespoons olive oil
3 tablespoons finely chopped onions
1 clove garlic, minced
4 tablespoons dry bread crumbs
1 tablespoon minced parsley

Peel the eggplant and cut in ½-inch slices. Sprinkle with the salt and let stand 20 minutes. Drain and dry well. Heat the oil in a skillet, add the eggplant, and sauté until delicately browned on both sides. Remove and arrange on a hot serving dish. Sauté the onions in the skillet 2 minutes, add the garlic, bread crumbs, and parsley, and sauté 2 minutes, stirring almost constantly. Sprinkle over the eggplant.

Serves 4-6.

Variation

Mix 2 cups thinly sliced zucchini, sautéed for 10 minutes, with the eggplant. Add 1 cup sautéed mushrooms to bread crumb mixture.

AUBERGINES À LA VAUCANSON

Eggplant au Gratin

6 tablespoons butter
1 tablespoon finely chopped onion
Salt, freshly ground black pepper
2 pounds ripe tomatoes, skinned, seeded, and coarsely diced
3 tablespoons thick Béchamel Sauce (see recipe)
2 small eggplants, peeled and sliced lengthwise
Flour
Grated Swiss cheese

Melt 2 tablespoons butter in a saucepan, add the onion, season with salt and pepper, and cook, stirring frequently, until onion is golden. Add tomatoes and cook until soft. Mix in white sauce and 2 tablespoons butter.

Season eggplant slices with salt and pepper, dip in flour, and sauté in the remaining butter until tender. Arrange eggplant in layers in a buttered shallow baking dish, putting between each layer part of the tomato mixture and some grated Swiss cheese. Cover top layer with tomato mixture, sprinkle with cheese, and brown in a 450° oven 10 minutes.

Serves 6.

FLAMICHE AUX POIREAUX

Leek Pie

10 leeks (white part), sliced thin
2½ tablespoons butter
Salt, freshly ground white pepper
1 tablespoon flour
1½ cups light cream
2 tablespoons diced bacon
1 9-inch unbaked pie shell

Sauté leeks in 1 tablespoon butter until almost soft. Season with salt and pepper. Melt 1 tablespoon butter, blend in flour, and slowly add cream, stirring to the boiling point. Cook 5 minutes, or until thickened, stirring constantly. Sauté bacon until lightly cooked but not brown. Mix leeks with white sauce and bacon and simmer 4 minutes. Pour into pie shell, dot with remaining butter, and bake in a 400° oven 30 minutes or until crust is golden on the edges. Serve at once.

Serves 6.

OIGNONS FARCIS

Stuffed Onions

6 large sweet onions
¼ pound beef, ground
¼ pound sausage meat
2 tablespoons butter
2 tablespoons flour
1 cup beef or chicken stock
2 teaspoons brandy
1 teaspoon salt
¼ teaspoon freshly ground black pepper

Peel the onions, scoop out the centers and reserve. Stuff onions with a mixture of beef and sausage meat. Chop the scooped-out centers of the onions. Melt the butter in a skillet and brown the chopped onion, sprinkle with the flour, and mix in the stock, brandy, salt and pepper, stirring to the boiling point. Simmer 3 minutes, then pour into an ovenproof casserole. Arrange the onions in the sauce and bake in a 350° oven 1½ hours, basting with the sauce several times during the cooking period.

Serves 6.

CHAMPIGNONS SAUTÉS À LA LOCHOISE

Sautéed Mushrooms

2 tablespoons butter
¾ pound mushrooms, sliced
1 shallot, chopped
1 small clove garlic, chopped
1 teaspoon chopped parsley
2 tomatoes, skinned, seeded, and coarsely chopped
Salt, freshly ground black pepper

Melt the butter in a heavy skillet and sauté the mushrooms, shallot, garlic, parsley, and tomatoes over medium heat, seasoning to taste with salt and pepper. Cook until the liquid has almost completely evaporated.

Serves 2-3.

CHAMPIGNONS À LA BORDELAISE

Mushrooms, Bordeaux Style

- *2 pounds mushrooms*
- *2 tablespoons butter*
- *2 tablespoons olive oil*
- *3 tablespoons chopped shallots or onions*
- *1 teaspoon salt*
- *¼ teaspoon freshly ground black pepper*
- *1 tablespoon minced parsley*

Chop the stems of the mushrooms and slice the caps. Heat the butter with the oil in a skillet, add the sliced mushrooms, and sauté over high heat until browned and crisp. Mix in the stems, shallots, salt and pepper, reduce heat, and sauté over low heat 5 minutes. Adjust seasoning, sprinkle with parsley, and serve with additional browned butter, if desired.

Serves 6-8.

CHAMPIGNONS SAUTÉS À LA TOURAINE

Sautéed Mushrooms and Tomatoes

- *1 pound mushrooms*
- *3 tablespoons butter*
- *1 clove garlic, minced*
- *3 tomatoes, skinned and chopped*
- *1½ teaspoons salt*
- *½ teaspoon freshly ground black pepper*
- *1 tablespoon minced parsley*

Slice the mushrooms, melt the butter, and sauté the mushrooms 3 minutes. Stir in the garlic, tomatoes, salt, pepper, and parsley and cook over medium heat 15 minutes or until mixture is fairly dry, stirring often to prevent burning.

Serves 4-6.

PURÉE DES OIGNONS

Onion Purée

1 pound onions, sliced
1 tablespoon butter
2 cups thick cream sauce
Salt, freshly ground white pepper
¼ teaspoon sugar
1 tablespoon tomato paste
2 tablespoons cream

Blanch the onions in boiling water 2 minutes. Drain well. Sauté in butter until soft but not brown. Mash. Combine with cream sauce, salt and pepper to taste, sugar, tomato paste, and cream. Force mixture through a fine sieve and cook the purée until it is the consistency of a thick sauce.

Serves 4.

PETITS POIS BONNE FEMME

Peas with Bacon

4 slices bacon, diced
½ cup thinly sliced scallions (green onions)
2 tablespoons flour
½ teaspoon salt
⅛ teaspoon white pepper
1½ cups hot beef broth
2 pounds green peas, shelled, or 2 packages frozen, thawed

Brown the bacon and scallions in a skillet; pour off all but 1 tablespoon fat. Blend in the flour, salt and pepper. Add the broth gradually, stirring steadily to the boiling point. Add the peas; cover and cook over medium heat 20 minutes for fresh peas; 8 minutes for frozen.

Serves 4-6.

POMMES DE TERRE À LA LYONNAISE

Potatoes and Onions

4 large potatoes, about 2 pounds
5 tablespoons butter
1 cup thinly sliced onions
1½ teaspoons salt
⅛ teaspoon freshly ground white pepper
2 teaspoons minced parsley

Cook the potatoes, with skins on, until done but still firm. Drain, peel off skins, and slice crosswise. Melt 2 tablespoons butter in a skillet, add the onions, and sauté until golden brown. Remove. Add remaining butter to skillet and lightly brown the potatoes. Add onions, season with salt and pepper, and sauté another 3 minutes. Serve sprinkled with parsley.

Serves 4-6.

POMMES DE TERRE FARCIES

Stuffed Potatoes

6 Idaho potatoes
2 tablespoons butter
1 small onion, finely chopped
½ pound sausage meat
2 tablespoons chopped parsley
½ teaspoon salt
¼ teaspoon white pepper

Peel the potatoes and halve lengthwise. Scoop out a large piece from each half, leaving a shell with some raw potato in it. Cook the scooped-out portion in boiling salted water until tender. Mash well and combine with the butter, onion, sausage meat, parsley, salt and pepper. Fill the raw potatoes with the mixture. Arrange in a buttered baking dish and bake in a 350° oven 1 hour.

Serves 6-12.

PFLÜTTERS ALSACIENNE

Potato Puffs

2 pounds potatoes, peeled and boiled
2 tablespoons flour
2 eggs, beaten
1 clove garlic, crushed
2 tablespoons finely chopped parsley
1 tablespoon melted butter
Salt, freshly ground black pepper
Pinch nutmeg

Mash the potatoes and blend in the flour, eggs, garlic, parsley, melted butter, and seasonings and nutmeg to taste. Mix well together and put large tablespoons of the mixture in a buttered baking dish, not quite touching. Bake in a 325° oven 12 minutes, then put under a broiler to brown a little. Pour a little melted butter over the puffs and serve.

Serves 6-8.

GRATIN DAUPHINOIS

Crunchy Potatoes

2 pounds potatoes, peeled and sliced as thin as possible
Salt, freshly ground black pepper
⅛ teaspoon grated nutmeg
1½ cups light cream
2 tablespoons butter

Arrange the potatoes in a buttered shallow baking dish, sprinkling salt, pepper, and nutmeg between the layers. Add the cream and dot with small pieces of the butter. Bake in a 250° oven for 1½ hours or until the cream is almost absorbed and the potatoes brown.

Serves 4.

LA RÂPÉE

Potato-Cheese Pancakes

6 large raw potatoes, peeled and grated
1 cup heavy cream
2 tablespoons melted bacon fat
2 tablespoons grated Cheddar cheese
1½ teaspoons salt
½ teaspoon freshly ground black pepper
¼ cup oil

Mix well together the potatoes, cream, bacon fat, cheese, and salt and pepper.

Heat a little oil in a small skillet and spread a thin layer of the potato mixture over the bottom of the pan. Brown on the bottom, sprinkle top with a little oil, and brown under the broiler. Turn out and keep warm. Repeat until all potato mixture is used.

Makes about 24.

TOMATES SAUTÉES À LA PROVENÇALE

Sautéed Tomatoes, Provençal Fashion

4 tomatoes, halved and seeded
½ teaspoon salt
¼ teaspoon freshly ground black pepper
4 tablespoons oil
2 cloves garlic, finely chopped
2 tablespoons finely chopped parsley
2 tablespoons very coarse bread crumbs

Season the tomatoes with salt and pepper. Heat the oil in a skillet and sauté the tomatoes lightly on each side. Add garlic and cook 2 minutes. Transfer tomatoes to a hot serving dish and sprinkle with parsley. Add bread crumbs to oil remaining in skillet and sauté 2 minutes, or until crumbs are browned and oil absorbed. Sprinkle over tomatoes and serve.

Serves 4.

TOMATES FARCIES

Stuffed Tomatoes

- *6 large firm tomatoes*
- *4 tablespoons olive oil*
- *1 clove garlic, finely chopped*
- *2 tablespoons chopped scallions (green onions)*
- *2 tablespoons chopped parsley*
- *¼ pound mushrooms, chopped*
- *¾ teaspoon salt*
- *¼ teaspoon freshly ground black pepper*
- *½ cup dry bread crumbs*
- *4 tablespoons grated Swiss cheese*

Wash and dry the tomatoes and scoop out the centers. Chop the centers.

Heat 2 tablespoons oil in a skillet and sauté the garlic, scallions, parsley, and mushrooms 3 minutes. Mix in the chopped tomatoes; cook until fairly dry. Season with the salt and pepper and mix in the bread crumbs. Stuff the tomatoes with this mixture and arrange in a large, well-oiled casserole. Sprinkle with the cheese and brush with the remaining oil. Bake in a 350° oven 45 minutes, basting occasionally with the pan juices.

Serves 6.

TOMATES VAUCLUSIENNES

Tomatoes and Eggplant

- *1 eggplant*
- *3 teaspoons salt*
- *6 tablespoons olive oil*
- *6 tomatoes (2 pounds), skinned and chopped*
- *2 cloves garlic, minced*
- *¼ teaspoon basil*
- *½ teaspoon freshly ground black pepper*
- *½ cup dry bread crumbs*

Peel the eggplant and cut in ¼-inch slices lengthwise. Sprinkle with 1½ teaspoons salt and let stand 15 minutes. Drain and dry. Heat 2 tablespoons oil in a skillet and sauté eggplant until brown on both sides. Remove and put in a baking dish. Add 2 more tablespoons oil to the skillet, add the tomatoes, garlic, basil, pepper, and remaining salt and cook over low heat 20 minutes. Stir in ¼ cup bread crumbs and adjust seasoning. Spread tomato mixture over eggplant. Sprinkle remaining crumbs and oil on the top and bake in a 400° oven 35 minutes.

Serves 6-8.

ZUCCHINI PROVENÇALE

SAUTÉED ZUCCHINI

2 pounds zucchini
1 teaspoon salt
4 tablespoons olive oil
1 clove garlic, chopped
2 shallots, chopped
1 tablespoon chopped parsley
2 tablespoons dry bread crumbs

Cut the zucchini, with the skin on, into ½-inch thick slices. Sprinkle with salt and let stand ½ hour. Drain and dry. Sauté zucchini in hot oil in a skillet, putting in only a few slices at a time. Turn slices often. When both sides are browned, transfer to a hot platter. When all zucchini slices have been browned, add the garlic, shallots, parsley, and bread crumbs to the oil remaining in the skillet. Sauté a minute, taking care the garlic does not burn. Sprinkle crumb mixture over the zucchini.

Serves 4.

LA BROYE

Cornmeal Pudding

2½ cups beef stock
1 cup cornmeal
Bacon fat

Bring stock to a boil in a saucepan. Pour a little over the cornmeal and stir hard to dissolve all lumps. Gradually add the rest of the stock, return to pan, and cook mixture 10 minutes or until thick. Spread on a wooden board in a ½-inch layer and cool. Cut into squares and brown on each side in bacon fat. Serve with meats instead of potatoes.

Note: Use either white or yellow cornmeal. The water-ground, somewhat coarse, white is better.

Serves 6.

LÉGUMES À LA NIVERNAISE

Mixed Vegetables in Cream

6 tablespoons butter
1 cup shredded lettuce
8 scallions, sliced
4 carrots, sliced
2 pounds shelled green peas or 2 packages frozen, thawed
1¼ teaspoons salt
½ teaspoon sugar
¼ cup water
½ cup heavy cream

Melt the butter in a saucepan and add the lettuce, scallions, carrots, peas, salt, sugar, and water. Bring to a boil, cover, and cook over low heat 20 minutes, shaking pan frequently so vegetables do not stick and burn. Stir in cream and cook over high heat 2 minutes. Taste for seasoning.

Serves 6-8.

SALADE DE TOMATES, NIÇOISE

Riviera Tomato Salad

4 firm ripe tomatoes, skinned and thinly sliced
1 red onion, thinly sliced
1 teaspoon salt
½ teaspoon freshly ground black pepper
3 tablespoons chopped dill
3 tablespoons wine vinegar
½ cup olive oil

Arrange alternate overlapping slices of tomato and onion on 6 salad plates. Put the salt, pepper, dill, vinegar, and oil in a screw-topped jar and shake well. Pour over the tomatoes and onions and chill for 1 hour before serving.

Serves 6.

SALADE DE CHOU-FLEUR, LANDAISE

Cauliflower Salad

1 firm head cauliflower
½ cup French dressing
1 boiled beet
1 small green pepper, cut in rings
2 tablespoons butter

Break the cauliflower into flowerets and cook in salted water until tender but still firm. Drain well. While still warm pour over the flowerets 6 tablespoons French dressing. Slice beet into a bowl. Sauté green pepper rings in the butter for 2 minutes on each side. Add to beet and toss well with French dressing. To serve, arrange beet slices and pepper rings alternately on top of cauliflower to make a decorative pattern. Serve without chilling.

Serves 4.

Sauces

Sauces

FONDS BLANC

WHITE STOCK

1½ pounds veal bones
3 quarts water
2 teaspoons salt
2 whole onions
2 carrots
3 sprigs parsley
1 bay leaf
¼ teaspoon marjoram

Cover the bones with water; bring to a boil and cook 10 minutes. Drain, carefully removing the scum.

Combine the bones, 3 quarts water, salt, onions, carrots, parsley, bay leaf, and marjoram. Bring to a boil, cover loosely, and cook over low heat 3 hours. Strain, cool, and remove fat. Pour into jars, cover tightly, and refrigerate or freeze until needed. Use canned chicken broth as a possible substitute.

SAUCE BÉCHAMEL

WHITE SAUCE

3 cups milk (or 1½ cups milk and 1½ cups White Stock—see recipe)
3 tablespoons minced onion
1 bay leaf
4 tablespoons butter
⅓ cup flour
½ teaspoon salt
Dash white pepper

Bring the milk (or milk and stock), onion, and bay leaf to a boil. Let stand 15 minutes and strain.

Melt the butter in a saucepan; blend in the flour, until flour turns golden. Gradually add the strained liquid stirring constantly to the boiling point. Stir in the salt and pepper. Cook over low heat 20 minutes, stirring frequently; strain.

Makes about 2 cups.

Use as a base for other white sauces or with creamed dishes.

Note: For fish dishes, you may use bottled clam juice as part of the liquid.

SAUCE NANTUA

SEAFOOD SAUCE (for fish or seafood)

½ cup shrimp or lobster
1 cup Béchamel Sauce (see recipe)
¼ cup heavy cream

Purée ¼ cup shrimp or lobster in an electric blender or chop to a paste. Coarsely chop the remaining ¼ cup. Cook the Béchamel Sauce and cream over low heat for 5 minutes, but do not let boil. Stir in the seafood. Taste for seasoning, heat, but do not let boil.

Makes about 1½ cups.

SAUCE SOUBISE

ONION SAUCE (for sweetbreads, veal, or fish)

1 cup minced onions
3 tablespoons butter
2 cups Béchamel Sauce (see recipe)
1 cup heavy cream

Pour boiling water over the onions and let stand 5 minutes; drain. Cook the onions in the butter over low heat until soft, but do not let brown. Add Béchamel Sauce; cook 15 minutes. Slowly stir in cream; strain. Correct seasoning.

Makes about 2¾ cups.

SAUCE ESPAGNOLE

Brown Sauce

2 tablespoons butter
¼ cup minced shallots or onions
1 tablespoon flour
2 cups beef broth
⅛ teaspoon pepper
⅛ teaspoon thyme
1 bay leaf
2 teaspoons tomato paste

Melt the butter in a saucepan; sauté shallots for 5 minutes; stir in the flour and cook over low heat, stirring constantly until browned. Gradually add the broth, stirring until the boiling point. Add the pepper, thyme, bay leaf, and tomato paste. Cook over low heat 20 minutes. Strain. Use as a base for other sauces.

Makes 1½ cups.

SAUCE BORDELAISE

(for steak or roast beef)

Large marrow bone
2 tablespoons minced shallots or onions
¼ cup dry red wine
1 cup Brown Sauce (see recipe)
1 tablespoon cognac
1 teaspoon minced parsley

Have the butcher crack the bone; carefully remove the marrow. (You need about 3 tablespoons.) Dice it and place in lukewarm water for 5 minutes, then drain.

Cook the shallots and wine for 5 minutes. Stir in the Brown Sauce and cognac; cook over low heat 10 minutes. Add the marrow and parsley just before serving. Heat. Correct seasoning.

Makes about 1¼ cups.

SAUCE LYONNAISE

(for game or beef)

¼ cup minced onions
2 tablespoons butter
1 cup dry white wine
1½ cups Brown Sauce (see recipe)

Sauté the onions in the butter 10 minutes. Add wine and Brown Sauce; cook over low heat 5 minutes.

Makes 2 cups.

SAUCE ROBERT

(for pork or ham)

3 tablespoons minced onions
2 tablespoons butter
¼ cup wine vinegar
1 cup Brown Sauce (see recipe)
¼ cup chopped gherkins
1 teaspoon prepared mustard
2 teaspoons minced parsley

Sauté the onions in the butter for 5 minutes; add the vinegar and cook until reduced to half. Add the Brown Sauce and cook over low heat 15 minutes. Stir in the gherkins, mustard, and parsley just before serving.

Makes about 1⅓ cups.

SAUCE ROUENNAISE

(for wild or domestic duck)

4 duck livers or 8 chicken livers
3 tablespoons minced onions
1 tablespoon butter
¼ cup dry red wine
1½ cups Brown Sauce (see recipe)
1 tablespoon cognac

Wash the livers carefully, removing any discolored areas. Purée the livers in a blender or force through a fine sieve. Refrigerate until needed.

Sauté the onions in the butter for 5 minutes. Add the wine and cook until reduced to half. Stir in the Brown Sauce and cognac; cook over low heat 10 minutes. Just before serving, mix ¼ cup of the hot sauce with the liver. Return to the saucepan; heat but do not let boil. (This is an extremely rich sauce.)

Makes about 1¾ cups.

SAUCE BÉARNAISE

(for beef or fish)

3 tablespoons tarragon vinegar
¾ cup dry white wine
2 peppercorns
1 tablespoon finely chopped shallots or onion
1 tablespoon finely chopped fresh tarragon or 1 teaspoon dried
1 tablespoon finely chopped fresh chervil or 1 teaspoon dried
3 egg yolks
½ teaspoon salt
1 cup melted butter
2 teaspoons minced parsley
Dash cayenne pepper

Combine the vinegar, wine, peppercorns, shallots, tarragon, and chervil in a saucepan; cook over low heat until reduced to half. Beat the egg yolks and salt in a bowl; gradually add the wine mixture, beating steadily to prevent curdling. Still beating steadily, gradually add the butter until the mixture is the consistency of very thick cream. Place over hot water and beat for a minute. Strain and add the parsley and cayenne pepper. If fresh herbs are used, add 1 teaspoon of each, chopped before serving.

Makes about 1½ cups.

For a darker sauce, called Valoise, to serve with eggs and broiled chicken, 1 teaspoon of *Glace de Viande* or meat extract may be added.

SAUCE RAVIGOTE

(for fish)

2 egg yolks
1 cup hot water
4 tablespoons butter
1 tablespoon flour
3 tablespoons tarragon vinegar
2 tablespoons minced shallots or onion
½ teaspoon salt
⅛ teaspoon freshly ground black pepper
1 teaspoon prepared mustard
1 teaspoon chopped fresh chervil or ⅛ teaspoon dried
1 teaspoon chopped fresh tarragon or ⅛ teaspoon dried
2 teaspoons chopped chives

Beat the egg yolks and gradually add the hot water, stirring steadily to prevent curdling. Melt 1 tablespoon of butter in a saucepan; stir in the flour and then the yolk mixture all at once. Stir steadily to the boiling point but do not let boil. Add remaining butter in small pieces, mixing steadily.

Cook the vinegar and shallots until reduced to half. Strain. Add to the sauce with the salt, pepper, mustard, chervil, tarragon, and chives.

Note: If dried herbs are used, soak in hot water for 10 minutes before adding.

Makes about 1½ cups.

BEURRE À LA MEUNIÈRE

MEUNIÈRE BUTTER (for fish or shellfish)

¼ pound butter
2 tablespoons lemon juice
2 teaspoons minced parsley

Melt the butter and cook over low heat until brown. Stir in the lemon juice and parsley.

Makes about ½ cup.

SAUCE NIÇOISE

(for cold shellfish or fish)

½ cup finely chopped green pepper
1 tablespoon tomato paste
⅛ teaspoon minced garlic
1 teaspoon minced fresh tarragon
1½ cups mayonnaise

Mix all ingredients together.
Makes about 1¾ cups.

Desserts

Desserts

CLAFOUTIS LIMOUSIN

CHERRY PUDDING CAKE

1 cup light cream
1½ cups milk
⅔ cup sifted flour
⅔ cup sifted confectioners' sugar
½ teaspoon salt
4 eggs
1 pound black cherries, pitted, or 2½ cups canned, drained black cherries

Put the cream and milk in a pan and scald. Cool. Sift the flour, sugar, and salt into a bowl. Beat the eggs. Make a well in the center of the flour and pour the beaten eggs and cooled milk mixture into it. Gradually work in the flour with a wooden spoon, beating until very smooth. Mix in the cherries.

Pour into a well-buttered 2-quart soufflé dish or baking dish and bake in a preheated 400° oven 35 minutes or until set and delicately browned on top. Sprinkle with confectioners' sugar and serve hot or cold.

Serves 6-8.

BABA AU RHUM

RUM CAKE

CAKE
½ envelope yeast
¼ cup lukewarm water
1 cup sifted flour
2 eggs
2 tablespoons heavy cream
⅓ cup sugar
¼ teaspoon salt
¼ cup softened butter
⅓ cup raisins
¼ cup chopped citron
¼ cup currants
Pinch of saffron

SYRUP
½ cup sugar
4 tablespoons water
2 tablespoons rum

Dissolve the yeast in the water. Add to the flour with the eggs and cream; mix with the hands 3 minutes. Form into a ball. Cover and let rise in a warm place until doubled in bulk. Punch down and add 1 teaspoon sugar, the salt, and softened butter and beat vigorously 5 minutes. Mix in the remaining cup sugar, the raisins, citron, currants, and saffron. Place in a buttered 7-inch tube pan, cover with a cloth, and let rise in a warm place until doubled in bulk. Bake in a preheated 375° oven 50 minutes or until browned. Meanwhile, boil the ½ cup sugar and the water for 10 minutes. Stir in the rum and cool a little.

Carefully turn out the baba and pour the rum syrup over it. Let stand a few minutes. Serve hot or cold.

Serves 6-8.

BISCUIT DE SAVOIE

Spongecake

3 tablespoons melted butter
2 teaspoons flour
2 teaspoons sugar
4 egg yolks
¾ cup sugar
½ cup flour
½ cup potato flour
¼ teaspoon vanilla extract
4 egg whites

Coat the inside of a 9-inch ring mold with melted butter and chill in the refrigerator until the butter sets. Sprinkle a mixture of the flour and sugar over the butter, turn and shake the mold until well coated, then shake out excess.

Beat egg yolks and sugar until very thick and light. Sift together flour and potato flour and blend into egg-sugar mixture. Add vanilla and mix well. Beat the egg whites until stiff and add a small amount to the batter. Mix in thoroughly. Fold the remainder of the whites in gently. Pour into the prepared pan; bake in a preheated 325° oven 40 minutes or until top springs back when pressed with the finger. Remove from oven and let stand 15 minutes before turning out on a cake rack. Cool a few hours before serving.

GALETTE DE MÉNAGE

Family-Style Cake

2 cups flour
1 tablespoon sugar
½ teaspoon salt
½ cup warm milk
¾ cup softened butter
1 egg yolk
1 tablespoon water

Sift the flour onto a pastry board and make a well in the center. Into it put the sugar, salt, milk, and softened butter. Work in the flour with the finger tips until the dough forms a smooth ball. Allow to stand 45 minutes. Roll out ½ inch thick. Trace vertical and horizontal lines over the surface of the pastry with a sharp knife, so it is covered with a pattern of squares or rectangles. Use care so as not to cut through the pastry. Place on a buttered and floured cooky sheet and brush with the egg yolk beaten with the water. Bake in a preheated 450° oven 30 minutes, or until browned.

GALETTE STRASBOURGEOISE

Raisin Coffee Cake

½ envelope yeast
¼ cup lukewarm water
1 cup light cream, scalded
2 tablespoons butter
2 cups sifted flour
¼ cup sugar
¼ cup seeded raisins

Dissolve the yeast in the water.

Mix the cream and butter together until butter melts. Mix well with flour. Add sugar, raisins, and dissolved yeast. Mix with your hands for several minutes—the dough will be quite soft, almost a batter. Put in a deep buttered cake pan, cover, and let rise 2 hours. Bake in a preheated 450° oven 30 minutes or until browned. Cool.

CRÈME BRÛLÉE

Custard with Caramel Topping

6 egg yolks
⅓ cup sugar
3 cups heavy cream, scalded
2 teaspoons vanilla extract
½ cup light brown sugar, packed

Preheat oven to 325°.

Beat the egg yolks and sugar in a bowl. Gradually add the hot cream and vanilla, stirring steadily to prevent curdling. Strain into a 1½-quart soufflé or baking dish. Set in a shallow pan containing 1 inch of hot water. Bake 30 minutes or until a silver knife inserted in the center comes out clean. Chill.

The cream may be served as soon as the sugar caramelizes or chilled again. If you want to serve it hot, spread with the brown sugar just before serving. Set the dish in a shallow pan containing cracked ice or on a board. Place under the broiler until sugar melts and browns. Watch carefully to prevent burning. Serve at once or prepare a few hours in advance and chill.

Serves 6-8.

MOUSSE AU CHOCOLAT

Chocolate Mousse

4 1-ounce squares unsweetened chocolate
¾ cup sugar
¼ cup water
5 egg yolks
1 tablespoon brandy
5 egg whites

Melt the chocolate over hot water in the top of a double boiler. Add the sugar and water and stir until sugar dissolves. Beat the egg yolks; gradually beat in the chocolate mixture, stirring steadily. Stir in the brandy. Cool completely. Beat the egg whites until stiff. Fold into the chocolate mixture. Pour into 6-8 individual molds and chill in the refrigerator at least 12 hours (it will keep well for several days).

Serves 6-8.

MOUSSE AUX FRAMBOISES

Raspberry Mousse

1 envelope (tablespoon) gelatin
½ cup cold water
2 packages frozen raspberries, thawed
¼ cup sugar
2 egg whites
1½ cups heavy cream

Soften the gelatin in the water.

Drain the berries thoroughly and measure the juice. If necessary, add water to make 1 cup. Combine the juice and sugar in a saucepan; cook over low heat until syrupy. Add the berries; cook over low heat 10 minutes. Mix in the gelatin until dissolved. Force through a sieve. Cool.

Beat the egg whites until stiff but not dry. Fold into the raspberry mixture. Whip the cream lightly and add; beat the mixture until thick. Pour into a mold and chill until set.

Serves 6-8.

SOUFFLÉ GLACE AU CITRON

Frozen Lemon Soufflé

1 envelope (tablespoon) gelatin
¼ cup cold water
6 egg yolks
1 cup sugar
⅔ cup lemon juice
1 tablespoon grated lemon rind
4 egg whites
1½ cups heavy cream

Butter a band of waxed paper and fasten around the top of a 1-quart soufflé dish to form a collar extending ¾ inches over the top of the dish.

Soften the gelatin in the water. Beat the egg yolks and sugar until thick and light. Stir in the lemon juice; cook over low heat, beating steadily until thickened and hot but not boiling. Mix in the gelatin until dissolved and then the lemon rind. Remove from heat and cool, mixing occasionally.

Beat the egg whites until stiff but not dry; fold into the lemon mixture. Whip the cream and fold in. Slowly pour into the soufflé dish; the mixture will rise above the top of the dish. Freeze, then carefully remove the paper. Decorate the top with whipped cream and grated lemon rind, if desired.

Serves 8-10.

CRÊPES

Pancakes

2 cups milk
1 cup water
2 cups sifted flour
2 eggs
1 tablespoon salad oil
1 teaspoon salt
1 tablespoon brandy
2 tablespoons butter

Gradually add the milk and water to the flour, beating steadily until the batter is very smooth. Beat in the eggs, oil, salt, and brandy until very smooth. Chill 1 hour.

Heat a 6-inch skillet and lightly grease with butter. Pour a spoonful of batter into the pan and tilt pan so batter coats the entire surface—the layer of batter should be very thin. When browned, flip over with a spatula and cook on the other side. Add butter to pan and continue until all batter is used. As each *crêpe* is made, stack it and keep warm. To serve, fold *crêpes* in quarters, or roll. (You may spread each *crêpe* with jam before folding it, if you wish.) Sprinkle with sugar.

Makes about 16.

CRÈME FRITE

Cream Fritters

1 cup flour
½ cup cold water
2 cups milk
¼ teaspoon salt
8 tablespoons sugar
½ teaspoon grated lemon rind
2 egg yolks
¾ fine dry bread crumbs

Mix the flour and water to a smooth paste. Bring the milk to a boil; add the flour-and-water mixture, stirring steadily until well blended. Mix in the salt, 6 tablespoons sugar, and the lemon rind and cook over very low heat 15 minutes. Remove from the heat and allow to cool. Beat 1 egg yolk and stir into the cooled mixture. Pour into a buttered cake tin and chill thoroughly.

Beat the remaining egg yolk and the remaining sugar. Cut the chilled mixture into rounds or strips, dip in the sweetened egg yolk, roll in the crumbs, and fry in 370° deep fat until delicately browned, about 2 minutes.

Serves 6.

BEIGNETS DE POMMES

Apple Fritters

2 cups flour
½ teaspoon salt
2 eggs, separated
1 teaspoon brandy
1 cup milk
4 cooking apples, peeled, cored, and sliced in ⅛-inch-thick rounds
Fat for deep frying
Powdered sugar

Put the flour in a bowl. Make a well in the center and put in it the salt, egg yolks, and brandy. Work in the flour from sides to center until thoroughly mixed. Slowly add the milk, beating with a whisk, until the batter is smooth. Stiffly beat the egg whites and fold in. Dip the apple rounds in the batter and fry in 375° deep fat for 3 to 5 minutes. Sprinkle with powdered sugar and serve.

Serves 4.

PÂTE FEUILLETÉE

Puff Paste

1 pound sweet butter	*1 teaspoon salt*
4 cups flour	*1 cup ice water*

Shape the butter (reserving 2 tablespoons) into a flat square cake about ½ inch thick. Chill.

Sift the flour and salt into a bowl. With the fingers, work in the 2 tablespoons butter. Gradually add the water, mixing with the hand until it holds together in a pliable ball. It may not be necessary to add all the water. On a lightly floured surface, roll out the dough into a rectangle 10 inches long and ½ inch thick. Place the butter in the center and fold over 1 side and then the other, covering the butter completely. Press the edges together. Chill 20 minutes.

Place the dough on the floured surface with one of the pressed edges towards you. Roll out into a rectangle again, without letting the butter be exposed. Fold over into thirds, turn one open end towards you, and roll out again. (This is called a turn.) Fold into thirds and chill for 20 minutes. Repeat the rolling and chilling twice more, then use pastry as directed in recipes.

FLAKY PASTRY

2 cups sifted flour	*¾ cup shortening*
¾ teaspoon salt	*6 tablespoons ice water*

Sift the flour and salt into a bowl. Using a pastry blender or two knives, cut in ½ cup of the shortening until the consistency of coarse corn meal. Break up the remaining shortening and cut in until mixture is the size of peas. Sprinkle with a little water and toss with a fork, adding just enough water to make the flour mixture cling together. Wrap in a damp cloth and chill 30 minutes.

Divide dough in two, making one piece slightly larger than the other. On a lightly floured surface, roll out the larger piece as thin as possible. Fit into an ungreased 9-inch pie plate. Trim the edges. Brush edges with water or egg white. Fill with selected filling. Roll out the remaining pastry as thin as possible. Cut a few slits in the top. Cover the filling with the pastry. Press edges together on the rim to seal; fold edge of crust under bottom and flute or press with the tines of a fork. Bake as directed for each recipe.

TRUFFETTES DAUPHINOISSES

Chocolate Truffles

½ pound sweet chocolate
⅓ cup milk
¼ pound sweet butter
2 egg yolks, beaten
Grated unsweetened chocolate

Break the sweet chocolate into small pieces and combine with the milk. Place over hot water and cook, stirring frequently until melted. Stir in the butter until melted. Cool 10 minutes and mix in the egg yolks. Chill for 1 hour or until firm enough to handle. Shape into small walnut-sized balls and roll in the grated chocolate until heavily coated. Keep in a cool place.

Note: ½ cup ground almonds may be added to the chocolate mixture before chilling, if desired.

Makes about 36.

CONVERSION CHART

FOR WEIGHTS, MEASURES, AND TEMPERATURES

Weight Equivalents

American & British	*French*
1 oz.	30 grams
2 oz.	60 grams
8 oz.	240 grams
1 pound	480 grams

Liquid Equivalents

American		*British*		*French*
¼ cup	=	2 ounces	=	0.56 deciliters
⅓ cup	=	2½ ounces	=	0.75 deciliters
½ cup	=	4 ounces	=	1.13 deciliters
⅔ cup	=	5 ounces	=	1.5 deciliters
¾ cup	=	6 ounces	=	1.68 deciliters
1 cup	=	8 ounces	=	2.27 deciliters
2 cups	=	16 ounces	=	4.5 deciliters
1 quart	=	32 ounces	=	9 deciliters

Other Equivalents

American & British	*French*
1 pinch	1 pincée
1 teaspoon	1 cuillère à café
1 tablespoon	1 cuillère à soupe

Temperature Equivalents

American (Fahrenheit)	*British* (Regulo—Fahrenheit)	*French* (Centigrade)
225°	#¼	Doux 107
250°		
275°	#½	
300°	#1 (291°)	Moyen 140
325°	#2 (313)	
350°	#3 (336)	Assez Chaud 177
	#4 (358)	
375°	#5 (379)	
400°	#6 (403)	
425°	#7 (424)	Chaud 210
450°	#8 (446)	
475°	#9 (469)	Très Chaud 246

INDEX

Index

D

E

F

G

H

S

T

V

W

Y